Messages from Somewhere

Messages from Somewhere
Inspiring Stories of Life After 60
Copyright ©2001 by Harriet May Savitz. All rights reserved.
LTP–Published by Little Treasure Publications
www.littletreasurebooks.com

Book Design by Pneuma Books: Complete Publisher's Services
For complete information, call (410) 287-1235. http://www.pneumadesign.com/books/info.htm
Set in ITC Berkeley 14|19 pt. Titles set in Natalie 25 pt.

Printed in the United States of America on recycled paper
08 07 06 05 04 03 02 01 00   9 8 7 6 5 4 3 2 1

Publisher's Cataloging-in-Publication
(Provided by Quality Books, Inc.)

Savitz, Harriet May.
    Messages from somewhere : inspiring stories of life
after 60 / Harriet May Savitz.
    p. cm.
    LCCN 2001093263
    ISBN 0-9639838-5-7
    1. Savitz, Harriet May. 2. Aged--United States--
Psychology. 3. Women authors, American--20th century--
Biography. I. Title.

PS3569.A845M47 2001   813'.54
                    QBI01-701383

Messages from Somewhere

Inspiring Stories of Life After 60

Harriet May Savitz

Dedication

This book is dedicated to the people who inspire
and support me each and every day.

Ephraim Savitz
Liz and Steve, Jake and Ben Savitz
Beth and Todd, Ryan and Jenny Laliberte
Ira M. Blatstein

Acknowledgments

A special thanks to the many "spokes" who
keep my wheel turning.

Vincent & Rosemary Accurso and Mitch,
Dick & Missy Lee, Paula Lizzi, Ann Mulloy Ashmore,
Evelyn & Al Lopez, Judy Baca, Irene Maran,
Morrie Berman, Mary Mooney, Richard & Troy Bianchi,
Ron Munro, Edward B. Davenport, Donna Murray,
Gloria & Bill Delamar, Tony Murray Family,
Dollie & Joe DiMino, Terry & David Page, Anne Dumas,
Arlene Smith, Carol Franzwick, Eileen Spinelli,
Mary Freeman, Michael Syring, Ellie & Gar Garfunkle,
Ferida Wolff, Stella Garzarelli, Linda Hadley Hoffman,
David Hall, John Hayes, Susan & Michael Holland,
Dee Jones, Jean Leahy

Table of Contents

continued…

Introduction:
Messages From Somewhere

One year after cancer surgery, just as I felt my recovery was possible, my husband died in his sleep. He had been my security. He took care of the outside world while I told stories. He protected me from the real world while I sat at my computer, creating a world of fiction. He wasn't afraid of reality. He knew I was. The only place I felt safe and in control, was when I was writing, for there I could make life do as I pleased, except when a book decided it knew better and its characters would take me along for an adventurous ride.

After my husband's death, I couldn't look at my writing desk. It taunted me whenever I did. I didn't want to touch the papers piled on it, nor go near the jars of pencils and pens that were waiting. What was the sense? I had nothing more to say. My mind was empty, my heart broken. For the first time in my life, I felt hollow. All the words that had buzzed around in my head, all the ideas, all of the characters, the future plots, vanished. It was dark inside me. There were no lights of creativity. There was no hope. I didn't want to see anyone. I didn't want to drive my car. I didn't want to shop for food. I stopped functioning.

My husband had been proud of my writing career. He bought me my first typewriter, and built an office around it. He called me a writer before anyone else thought it. He understood there were things I didn't understand, like what went on in the kitchen, or the benefits of housecleaning. It was O.K. he'd say, because he couldn't write a book. And that was that.

He was the outside person, and I was the inside person, taking care of the pets, watering the plants, keeping the house together, and being there when he came home. While I sat in front of the typewriter, he had the car winterized, the tires checked, took care of the insurance payments, and many other things I didn't know existed.

"Go write," he would tell me on an off day. "You'll feel better." And I did.

I was more comfortable in my fiction world. Fiction had become my reality. Each time the characters came to life, they amazed me. How did that happen? One moment, I was shaping, changing, rewriting. The next moment, there they were, standing whole, with a movement of their own. How did I do it, or did I? Did it come from somewhere else, someone else? A higher being? A spiritual guide?

Sometimes I didn't want to see the stories. Sometimes I wished my mind would take a rest, go to sleep for a while.

Sometimes I wished I could close that third eye of the writer. But I was always thinking, because I was always writing, because there was always another story, another message to get out. I would tell my writing students, "Passion. There has to be passion in the book." For what else could hold you in isolation for days, sometimes months or years, but passion. And then there was the getting ready for the book. Each book had to have an entrance. No book deserved to be written under the same circumstances as the one before. It was like having a new friend to dinner. There was always extra fussing, perhaps a fancy tablecloth, and the good silverware. So it was with a book. One book demanded to be written on yellow legal pads, another needed a black ledger in which notebooks were placed. Another refused the ledger and insisted on shelves; yes, bookshelves had to be built, for this would be a series, and the different books had to be placed on shelves. None of my books would accept the writing circumstances of another. No, for each, it would have to be a new place, a new ledger, another bookshelf, a chair placed differently, different writing paper, a pen one time, a pencil another, or straight to the computer.

"I'm getting ready for a book," I would tell someone. Their eyes would question, "How do you get ready?" It was best they didn't ask, because I couldn't tell them. It just meant much movement and searching and adjusting until it felt right. I was like a landlord getting ready for a new tenant. At last, the book was ready to move in.

Each book gave something and took something. "Be careful," I would tell new writers. "Protect the book while you write it, but also protect yourself from the book." The latter was more difficult. "Don't submerge yourself," I would caution as I submerged. "Don't let it take over your life completely," I would advise as it took over my life completely.

I was a mother, but always a writer. I was a wife, but always a writer. I was a friend, but always a writer. Those in my life knew it, they felt it, and so did I. And as I wrote, I thought of the "how" and the "why" more and more. Perhaps because as I grew older, the work seemed more intense, with a clearer message. *The message kept appearing over and over, throughout my stories. The power of a human being to survive.*

And then it was my turn. I had always thought I could write through anything. The true test arrived, when at the age of sixty, I had to face endometrial cancer, a major operation, and five weeks of radiation. I was accustomed to my body behaving so that I could write. Now I had no control over what my body did or what other people did to it. There were weeks of weakness, and weeks of terror, as my husband encouraged me to write. I would spend days sitting at the computer, feeling sorry for myself, my fingers on the keyboard, waiting, doubting. One day I suddenly realized I was not alone. My four cats and my dog were sitting in the room, staring at me. They looked as forlorn as I felt. Lately, I had not given them their expected attention. For a moment we looked into one another's eyes. Then one cat moved to my desk and purred beneath my hand as if to comfort me. Another jumped on my manuscript. Two sat on the window ledge by my side. My dog rubbed against my leg. They understood. They were consoling me. They were telling me I wasn't alone and it would be O.K. Each day, I would feel their eyes on me, as if they were expecting me to write, to write something, even if it was just about them. "Why not," they seemed to say. "We are always here for you. You tell everyone we are your best friends. You tell everyone we understand you better than anyone else. You tell others you never feel alone when you're writing, because we are here for you. Doesn't that make us important?" And so I turned on the computer and wrote about my animals. About all of my animals. About the cats and dogs and box turtles and birds, and every animal that had been in my life those sixty years. Each day I would sit in my office and write. Each day my four cats and my dog would sit with me. In those hours, I forgot about my illness. I only remembered the animals that had been in my life and now were encouraging me to work again.

It was a long recovery and I decided to write about that also, what I was living through, the radiation treatments, and the recovery of a coward who had to learn to be brave. I didn't write it for publication. I wrote it for myself.

But now, one year later, when my husband died, something in me died with him. My words failed to rescue me. My husband was gone, and with him, the glorious protection I had felt for 35 years. The outside world hit me in the face and knocked me out. I folded up. I turned off the computer and didn't turn it back on. I said good-bye to everyday living and sat in the house, avoiding the writing desk.

A friend accompanied me to a support group of people who had lost their spouses through death and divorce. They met in the basement of a church. Each week I would go and listen to others express their pain. Eventually, I talked about mine. It was a year before I told anyone in the group that I was a writer. I didn't feel like a writer. I wasn't living like one.

"Are you writing?" someone in the group asked.

"No," I responded

"Why not?"

"Because I have nothing to say."

And I didn't. Except to the support group each week.

It is appropriate that I tell you how I personally felt about writing. I looked upon it as a gift that had been given to me. Though I sometimes questioned how a book was delivered, or an essay, or a character, I understood some questions dared not be answered. One moment the page was blank, the next full. The conception of the story was never mine alone. It was delivered from somewhere. I was the facilitator, the story-teller, the middle-person. As I accepted the gift of creativity, I now accepted its leaving. What had been, was gone. In its place, emptiness. My soul felt like a dark cave without the bright lights it had known. "Is anyone in there?" I asked in the night. "Anyone at all?"

One middle of the night, after a year in the support group, I awoke, and there was a voice in my head. It was a new voice, unlike any I had heard before. Though it was an older voice, it held a fresh vibrancy. An excitement. An eagerness to be heard. The voice and the words kept coming, and I jumped out of bed. I hadn't heard anything in so long. I thought I would never hear a voice again. I turned on the computer and began to work. It was as if I were taking dictation. The words spilled out, first one essay, then another, and another. As if they had also been waiting, rushing toward their entrance. When I fell asleep that night, exhausted from hours of typing, I could only wonder. Would that voice return?

The next night, it did. Night after night, more essays, more ideas, more words. The essays would eventually become a published book. They were about my life during the year of silence, during the changes, during the illness, during the loss, during the time when I thought there was nothing left in me. The essays were delivered, six, sometimes seven at a time.

I raced to take down the words, afraid each day that the voice would disappear. I didn't know if what I was writing was good. I didn't care. All I knew is that the words were there again, spilling out, being delivered from somewhere, and I was anxious to begin each day, to eat, to drive, to talk, to do anything while I waited for another essay and another. It was the most exciting, mysterious writing experience of my life. It was as if I were just beginning. Where had this new voice come from? Who did it belong to? These essays, complete in first draft, who had composed them? Did I in my subconscious during my year of silence, or were they a gift?

I no longer am afraid that the messages from inside will stop, nor the voice be silenced. There might be bad times and frightening times ahead, but I understand now that if I am patient, one morning I shall awake, and there will be a character out of nowhere, a plot that must be explored, some phrases floating about. I know that they will come as they have always come, unexpected.

From somewhere.

Family

BOOK ONE

A Good Call

I want this to be a good telephone call. My son, Steve, has called. I haven't seen him in awhile. I miss him. I need to see his face in front of me. I want to put my arms around him, as if he were a little boy. I want to tell him that even though he is in his thirties and a grown man, the little boy in him comes alive when I see him. But I want this to be a good call. No pressure. No guilt. No whining.

I remember calling my parents. Sometimes the calls weren't good. I hung up feeling guilty about this or that. Not visiting enough. Not calling enough. Not doing one thing or another enough. I promised myself I would not do that to my children. After all, I was a liberated woman, a grandmother of the nineties. Much more aware, more sensitized, more independent than those of yesteryear.

So I want this to be a good call. I talk about the weather, about my work, about his job, about my grandchildren, Jake and Ben, and my daughter-in-law, Liz, as well as politics, and any interesting topics of the day. I try to be pleasant, and push down the words, "I miss you." I suffocate the plea, "I need to see you." I keep silent the complaint, "Of course I know you're busy, but I truly don't care. I'm up to my ears in busy people. I want to see your face like I want to see tomorrow's sunrise, or better yet, like I need to breathe."

The words fight with me and I feel them winning, but I want this to be a good call. I know all the reasons I shouldn't say what I want to say. I know it is natural for children to leave their parents. I realize it is the way it's supposed to be, that they form their own families. I understand that a husband's loyalty is to his wife first, a wife's loyalty to her husband. I read the books. I was going to be different. A today's woman. Self-sufficient. Needing nothing but my ability to make it on my own two feet.

But I've run out of strength and resolve. The call has lasted too long. My self-control is ebbing.

"I miss you," I wail into the telephone. "How long do I have to wait until I see your face?"

Just like any mother from the beginning of time.

~

Joe Comes Home

(THE WAY IT WAS)

It was a foggy night when it began, the drizzle light and haunting. We stood in a group like a dozen tiny damp sparrows, under the wide sky above, eyes upward, waiting, searching the darkness for the lights of the airplane that would bring Joe back to us.

Joe was coming home from the Vietnam War, and we had gathered at the airport; wife, mother and father, sister and brother, cousins and nephews, and friends. No one cared that hours had drifted by and it was now five in the morning. No one noticed that the rain splashed gently on our faces. All we did notice was the clock, the wristwatch, the time of the approaching flights called out on the loudspeaker.

Joe had spent a year over there, dodging bullets, not sure of the next day, of the next moment. We each had spent the year differently. Joe's wife waiting, his parents hoping, the children of his brothers and sisters wondering where Joe had gone, his friends writing, keeping in touch, reaching out across the miles of separation.

I remembered the letters, the jokes, the tries at lightness.

"Life's not the same without you," we'd say.

"Death is all around," he'd answer.

"Here are some salt water taffies from the shore."

"I smell the ocean," he'd recall.

"We went to a great movie last night…"

"I nearly got it today," we read as our hearts dropped.

Someone was always missing from the family dinners that year, when big dishes of food were spread across the table and we would break bread and share conversation. The chair not filled would stare at us and remind us of Joe.

At Christmas, when the tree went up, no one could bear to look at it for awhile, though presents were underneath waiting for Joe. When the New Year approached, we recalled the last New Year and the fond farewell when he left. Tears and the anguish returned.

We read the newspapers a lot that year… and listened carefully to the news. We knew he was in the thick of it. We shut our ears to the casualties and prayed… not him.

"The push is on," he'd write. "Each day gets worse."

"A couple more weeks," we'd answer. "Hang on, tiger." Our answers seemed inadequate, and so we prayed some more.

Suddenly my mind returned to the present as an excited

voice shouted, "Look… look over there!"

We all stood there in confusion while Joe approached. His wife reached him first, and then we were there, each one of us, and then all of us at once, in the center of the airport terminal, hugging him, reaching for him, touching his hair, shaking his hands, round and round again, tears, laughter, giggling, children jumping at his heels. Joe in the center saying, "Gosh, holy cow," shaking his head, not believing it was over, all over at last.

And then we stopped, all of us at once, and there was silence. He looked at us one by one, his eyes going over each of our faces, looking so deeply that it made me shiver. Silently, we looked at him, just as we would look at a newborn baby. Was he all there… all in place… no wounds… no scratches?

And then we were back at his home, and Joe was in his T-shirt standing at the sink saying, "Boy, water from a spigot," like it was some wonderful invention. "We got it from a can," he explained.

Click, click went the television dials. "I'm not listening," he'd laugh. "Just turning the channels. It feels so great." And then sinking a cigarette into an ashtray. "So much dying," he said quietly. "So many friends."

We fell silent watching the sadness fill his eyes. In that moment, as thoughts of the war crept over his face, he isolated himself and we all felt it. We felt him drift, but none of us was going to let him get away again, and so we enclosed him in the safety of all he had left behind.

"Grandpop's waiting to see you," someone said. Grandpop was 90 years old, and waiting for Joe the past year was his reason to live.

"Three babies born. You're an uncle three times," a sister boasted. She ruffled his hair, the sad look left his eyes and he was back with us, laughing, his hands constantly reaching out to touch us as he talked.

The aroma of bacon and coffee filled the room. It was time for breakfast. Someone turned on the radio. The men started chatting in groups. The women puttered around in the kitchen. Everything seemed just as it should be.

Joe was home at last.

—

Learning About Love

I am 67 and I am still learning about love. When I was younger, I loved most everything. I loved chocolate sundaes, dancing, my new typewriter. Also included on my list of loving were my parents, my husband, my children, and my pets. I loved each day, and the busyness of it, and I loved filling it with challenges. "I love this," I would say freely. And then the next minute I would love something else. There seemed no limit to the loving. It came so easily and there was so much to love.

But now I am more careful about my love supply. I know what it is like to love and lose a partner. The loving becomes painful. I know what it is like to love and lose a friend. The loving leaves an ache somewhere inside. I know what it is like to make a mistake about those I loved. Perhaps they didn't deserve the gift I offered… I have wasted my love, thrown it away, misplaced it, used it, and misused it. And often, when I think it has gone forever, love surprises me by returning, stronger than ever and with a larger supply. As if it were off somewhere preparing for the shortage.

I know I would learn something if love could answer a few questions. One would be, "Where do you come from when you enter without knocking, and where do you go when you leave without warning?" The other, "How do I keep you by my side?" I see love in people my age as they crochet afghans for their children, stitching their love into a pattern. I see it in hours spent waiting for a telephone call, a visit, a loving reminder that they are needed. People fall in love and out of it, love desperately, love eternally. The words, "I love you" can shake a dynasty, affect worldly decisions, change one's lifetime. At this end of my calendar years, I know no more about love than I did at the beginning. Except that I dare not be without it.

I was recovering from a stomach virus at my daughter's house. And feeling quite sorry for myself. Television annoyed me. I was impatient with well-wishers on the telephone. I didn't want to look out the window and watch other people enjoy the day. I thought of all the bleak things I could remember and piled them up in front of me. One day passed into two. Reading material lay scattered on the bed, but remained ignored. I had more important matters to attend. Self-pity was one of them. I felt old, spent, used-up, discarded, and mean. I was angry at my body, at my age, at all the things I hoped yet to do, but couldn't, at the energy that played tricks on me, and at the unpredictability of life. Such as a virus attacking without warning and claiming victory.

On the third day, as I lay on the pillow, realizing that I felt better but was still unwilling to re-enter life's merry-go-round with all its responsibilities, a paper airplane glided into the room and landed beside me on the bed. I looked up. The room was empty. I picked up the airplane and inspected it. A message written on its wings said, "Get well soon Grandmom. I love you. Ryan."

I heard activity outside the room. A snowstorm was brewing. Everyone was in the attic getting out sleds and boots. I left the bed and walked toward the doorway, carrying my paper airplane.

It was time to re-enter the world. Love led the way.

—

Perfect Moments

Just give me a few boats sailing on the marina, a blue sky dusted with clouds, and seagulls hovering overhead. A breeze that knows how to be gentle. And I think, "What a perfect moment."

And then I recall other perfect moments. Sitting with a three-year-old grandson, a breakfast tray in front of us, his cereal and mine waiting, the television screen showing cartoons. An understanding silence between us. His chubby hands rest on mine. Perfection.

And there are other times like this. A dinner table filled with children, laughter, reminiscing, and telling stories that make us forget the food in front of us. We laugh so much. I want to hold the moment forever. We forget the petty things, the work things, the every day pressures, and for that hour or two, the outside world must wait. We are filling up the emptiness with family.

And there are other moments like this. A grandson, ten years old, dances with me in his bedroom to the music of his generation. We are united in that moment, old and young, hands and legs moving to the beat, no differences that we can recognize. If there is more to the world, at this moment, I need none of it.

Perfect moments. We each have them, so many times over. A visit from a friend whose words heal and warm the soul. Confiding, sharing, trusting. Years of each becoming part of the other.

More moments gather to be remembered. A day well spent, the chores ahead at sunrise now completed, a sense of accomplishment, of fulfillment. I tuck the flowers away for the Fall, and store the rocking chairs in the garage for the Winter. I put the warm blanket beneath the outdoor couch so two stray cats have shelter. A glance toward Main Street at the end of the day offers me an orange-red sunset. It rests as a large halo over the stores.

A knock on the door and a surprise guest, someone unexpected and yet missed, standing there smiling, asking, "Is this a good time to visit?" Oh yes, for this person it's always a good time. And when her visit comes to an end, the house eagerly holds the good feelings she leaves behind. The moment lingers.

Perfect moments. They fly about like butterflies, difficult to catch, and yet, when they decide to pay you a call, one dare not miss the opportunity.

My granddaughter is dressed for her entry into first grade.

She shines with anticipation, her dark hair and eyes glistening, sensing something wondrous is about to happen. I share the excitement. The moment lasts long after she boards the school bus.

We drive down a street and the trees on either side curve toward the center, forming a leafy umbrella overhead. It is quiet in the car. Nothing dare intrude on this autumn-like perfection, not even conversation.

A piece of sea glass washes ashore and takes its place among my memories. It is smoothed from the ocean and delivered at my feet. The shade of blue bursts from the sand. I add it to my sea glass jar to look upon in Winter. It will seem even more perfect then.

No money exchanges hands during these moments etched in my mind. No monetary reward is given. Sometimes, not even a word of appreciation is offered to acknowledge these swiftly passing treasures. And yet they remain, loyally waiting to be revisited and savored again.

My daughter is working around the kitchen. She is bald from chemotherapy treatments. She is fighting breast cancer. Her hair is growing back, small black wisps line her scalp. Eyebrows and eyelashes are reappearing. Without the full black tresses framing her face, I notice the gentle slope of her chin, the skin, smooth and healthy, the clear blue eyes, bright with hope. Her beauty stands undaunted in the face of this new challenge. She flashes a smile in my direction and it defies description. I am renewed.

And it is another perfect moment.

~

Somewhere, Babe Ruth is Smiling

They were two chairs from Yankee Stadium, #15 and #22, and they sat in the basement of his grandparents' home for years, unnoticed. Now and then, family members would come upon them and be told the story of how they were purchased. It seems when Yankee Stadium was rebuilt in the early seventies, thousands of these chairs were sold at a modest price. Fans sitting in #15 and #22 watched the likes of Babe Ruth, Mickey Mantle, and Lou Gehrig make baseball history. Perhaps one of them even caught a ball hit by one of the all-time baseball greats.

Someone approached my son-in-law about buying the chairs. A generous offer was made and the family met in the basement to make the decision.

My grandson Ryan, a nine-year-old little leaguer, just returning from a baseball game wearing Lou Gehrig's #4 on his uniform, protested.

"I don't believe you're selling those chairs," he said. "You can't give them to someone else." He approached his grandfather, Bob who was the original owner of the chairs, his young eyes puzzled. "Why are you going to do that now?"

His parents, being much wiser about such things, explained that they could all make a healthy profit if they sold them. And now there was a buyer.

"You don't understand," Ryan was told as he persisted. Of course the grown-ups understood better. They were older. They were wiser. And they were certainly more realistic about financial matters. Everyone would benefit from the money received.

The chairs were lifted from the dust and cobwebs that had gathered about them, and placed in the center of the basement. They were chipped and worn. There were no fans sitting in them now, no cheers from the stadium that had surrounded them, no baseball greats to look down at with wonder. And yet they held a majesty that silenced even the adults for a few thoughtful moments.

The debate concentrated on whether to keep the chairs until they gathered more value or sell them now. But while the conversation continued, the little leaguer with the #4 on his shirt sat down in seat #22. The family had decided that it was the best thing that could have happened to them; that the money sure would come in handy and that a bird in the hand was worth two in the bush. While all of this was going on in the basement, the little leaguer began to cry. He didn't usually cry in front of an audience. It made everyone uncomfortable.

"I think we'd better go upstairs," his father said. The discussion was over. The decision made. The chairs would be sold.

But his son didn't move. It was as if Ryan were glued to the chair. "I can't get up," he said. It seemed he couldn't, even if he tried.

It was his grandfather who approached the boy. "Would you explain to me why you are so upset?" he asked.

They were grown-up words that came from Ryan's mouth when he spoke, as if they were delivered from somewhere else. "The people sitting in these seats got to see them all, the great ones, Gehrig, and Mantle and Ruth. Right from this seat." His young hands caressed the chair. "Sitting here, I know just what they felt like," Ryan said. "What a great feeling."

Of course everyone knew the wise thing to do, and they knew the realistic thing to do. And the prudent thing to do. But no one wanted to remove this young baseball player from his chair, especially his grandfather who remembered what it was like to be that young and that in love with baseball.

It was Ryan's chair now. Everybody in the basement realized it. And they finally understood what he was trying to tell them. There wasn't enough money in the world to buy seat #22 now that Ryan had found it, and there wasn't enough money in the world to equal the look on Ryan's face when he threw his arms around his grandfather to thank him.

That night a nine-year-old boy wearing #4 on his baseball shirt took home Yankee Stadium seat #22.

And somewhere, Babe Ruth is smiling.

~

The Chocolate-Covered Cherry

The children and I didn't think it unusual. We accepted it as just another part of my husband's personality; the uncontrollable but lovable gambler's passion, his wild streak, his ability to make friends and keep them, his acceptance of life as it was, and his precarious health problems.

He would bring home a chocolate-covered cherry, sometimes two or three, sometimes a dozen, for my young daughter Beth. She would squeal with delight as toddlers do, and bathe herself in chocolate; her fingers and cheeks, forehead and lips, smothered in the treat.

The chocolate-covered cherry tradition continued through life. When Beth was a child and on his knee, my husband found it easy to win over my daughter with the sweet gift. But as she grew older and needed deeper things, and life twisted and turned as it does for all of us when we are growing, the chocolate-covered cherry arrived with very little notice. Sometimes it was gobbled up. Sometimes it was left uneaten. During teenage years, it was all but forgotten.

When Beth married and had a child of her own, the chocolate-covered cherry reappeared. It showed up at the end of her day when she was tired from child-tending. It showed up on days when she thought she was forgotten by everyone. Her father remembered with the chocolate-covered cherry. His grandson Ryan also shared the benefits of this tradition.

Just days before he passed away, when granddaughter Jenny was only a few weeks old, my husband brought Beth a chocolate-covered cherry. She had put it in the refrigerator. Through the pain, shock and anger at his unexpected death, she forgot all about it. But one day Beth rediscovered the gift from her father. She told me later that she wrapped it carefully and put in the freezer, way in the back where it was safe. She kept it there for over four years. Periodically, she would visit the chocolate-covered cherry and her father at the same time.

She was working. A baby-sitter watched Jenny while Ryan was at baseball practice. Jenny wanted a sweet snack. They looked through the pantry cabinets, they looked in drawers, they looked in the refrigerator. Nothing seemed to satisfy her. Then they searched the freezer. Jenny had done that many times before, but this time, for some reason, she dug with her little hands way into the back.

It was Jenny who discovered the chocolate-covered cherry, unwrapped it, and popped it into her mouth.

We always regretted that her grandfather had never known his granddaughter and that she had never known his generous heart. But in his own way, he had seen to it that Jenny also received her own chocolate-covered cherry.

He had waited four years, until the time was right.

—

Friendship

BOOK TWO

A Friend Remembered

Lee was my friend. For many years, she called in the morning to say, "Hi, what's doin?" Her voice was warm, even when the morning wasn't. She introduced me to Christmas as simply as she introduced me to so many moments that filled her life. I remember the first time she brought over a box of homemade cookies and an invitation to see her newly decorated Christmas tree. I still savor the aroma of her kitchen during that December holiday.

We swapped holidays, my friend and I. I shared the lighting of my Chanukah candles with her. It became a yearly tradition; both families participating. We moved through the month of December with a surge of excitement, the lights in our windows facing one another.

But it wasn't just hoopla and gift- giving between us. There was special meaning in each candle lit, in the circle of friends gathered around the Christmas tree, and in each tenderly baked cookie. My friend brought a significance to Christmas and to Chanukah, that I had never experienced before. Her curiosity to learn about my religion and its traditions touched me. What she learned she shared with others.

But then again, Lee believed in giving. Many of us close to her depended on her helping hand and on the fact that it was always there. At Cub Scout meetings, school functions, picnics, and parties. She wasn't president of this or that; she had no trophies celebrating her accomplishments. Hers was a quiet banner that waved silently as she offered kindness and compassion.

A killer called cancer silenced the laugh, the swimming, the swinging tennis racket, the sewing machine, and the giving. Through it all, she held onto her dignity and spit in the eye of the word, "terminal."

We buried her in the Fall. I made a silent vow to ignore the approaching holidays. But Lee would have none of that. Memories persisted of words and feelings we had shared, as the star was placed on her Christmas tree, as the last Chanukah candle burned. She would not let me forget or ignore the blending of our families and friends at this time of the year.

I baked the cookies in her cookie tins. I hung the Santa Claus she had made by my front door. I joined her family as they put the star on the tree, and they helped light the Chanukah candles.

During December, as the years pass, I feel Lee's presence

stronger than ever, urging all who knew her to keep holiday traditions alive and united in understanding.

Somehow, I know, she's around, still very much part of it all.

~

Banana Love

I love bananas. I eat at least a banana a day. I am always running to the store for bananas. I can run out of tea or eggs, but never bananas. I become frantic if I do.

Anne lives upstairs. Some would call her my tenant. I call her my dear friend. One day she arrived at my door with two banana breads in her hand. She knew I had been ill with a cold. "This will make you feel better," she said. "It's banana bread, without nuts." Custom-made. She knew I didn't eat nuts.

If it had bananas in it, it had to be good. I was right. But it was more than good. It was wonderful. It was superb. It was addictive.

I didn't know two banana breads could be eaten so quickly. I froze one and digested the other. Visitors came and noticed the banana bread sitting on the cake dish.

"I love banana bread," each said.

I was very careful to give out small slices. Eventually, I decided to put the bread out of sight, thereby saving myself the uncomfortable experience of sharing it.

One day, I looked in the freezer, and there was none left. I searched in bakeries for banana bread, but none were custom-made. All had nuts. And then one day Anne appeared. With two more loaves of banana bread. This time the weather had been violent. Snow and strong winds had kept me inside. "This will make you feel better," she said.

And it did. One loaf on the cake plate. One loaf in the freezer. But now something was happening. I felt it. I kept looking at the banana bread, fearful of the last slice. I was becoming dependent on the next two loaves. I couldn't expect Anne to keep delivering banana bread because it made me feel better. She would become a prisoner of her own creation. And what about her other life? Full-time job. Devoted mother and grandmother. I couldn't expect her to be the constant provider of my banana bread.

And yet, how could I do without it now? I had become dependent on its benefits. I ate a slice and relaxed. Another, and enjoyed. Yet another, and I reached enlightenment. The realist in me announced. "You can learn to make it yourself."

But I knew it wouldn't be the same. Anne had added her special ingredients. The friendship we shared was included in the recipe, along with her baking experience. This week I hurt my back. Anne arrived at the door with two loaves of banana bread. "You don't have to do this," I told her. "I'll find banana bread without nuts, somewhere. I know it's out there."

She just shook her head, smiled, and handed me the two loaves.

With love…

⁓

Beginnings

W e are three women in our sixties. Two are widows and are working. One has never married, but is committed to a long-term relationship. We are sitting in the living room, becoming friends. The television is playing but we pay no attention to it. We are conversing.

We speak of times past, but only to give perspective to our present and future. One has just purchased a house for the first time, by herself. She is not part of a couple. There is no "us" involved. She has made all the decisions... where and why. There is a future in this house. It will be her shore home, her runaway place.

The other has just retired. She thinks, "what now?" Her life has had many responsibilities. The burdens have lightened. Hours are her own. She could be selfish at this time in her life. This takes learning. She once was an artist. Perhaps she'll return to it. Or learn something new.

The third, myself, feels the need for a challenge. Discovery taunts me. "Have you used me at all lately?" it asks. Risk teases. "Why do you keep running away from me and playing it safe? Take a chance, you fool." Adventure won't keep quiet either. "I'm everywhere," it tells me daily. "Just peek outside that safe fortress you've built and find me."

We spend two hours talking to one another. We confide our dreams, and are not surprised that we dream in our sixties of new beginnings. We have not stopped searching for answers.

That night I can't sleep. The evening's conversation spins in my head. So I read Emerson's essays. He reminds me that though the body might show its age and have its limits, the mind is free and ageless.

Tonight my mind runs wild.

~

Dark Day Sent Away

Iknow it is a dark day as soon as I get out of bed. I didn't sleep restfully. Worries piled up in my head. Stuff has happened I can't forget. The problems are with me as I begin the morning. Like a load on my shoulders. Heavy. To add to my mood, the sky is cloudy and threatening. It is a dark day and I know I can't make it alone.

I reach for the telephone. I call a friend. We talk for an hour. I share my feelings. I cry. I protest, "Life isn't kind." She listens. She doesn't say much but she needn't. Listening is enough. It gets me through the morning.

But the dark day isn't finished with me. Some bad news trickles in. It eats away at my foundation. I need to reach out again. More tears are spilled. I can't believe they are there waiting. This friend advises, "Make a plan to get out of this so you can move forward." It is difficult to create a plan on a dark day, but with some help from a friend, I am able to do it. The day becomes a bit brighter.

I think about my plan for awhile. It gets me through the

early afternoon and then doubt surfaces. Perhaps I can't implement this plan. Maybe it will not work, or it will be a waste of time. I reach for the telephone again to call another friend. I do not wear my mask, the usual smiling, understanding, able-to-cope mask. That face folds like an accordion, as I confide my fears to the friend on the phone. "You think you have problems," she tells me. "Let me tell you mine, but promise you won't laugh." And then she shares her story.

Another friend offers the news, "My dear, I just read that in several trillion years our world as we know it will be over." We laugh together over the trillion year prophecy. Laughter lightens the dark day.

By the end of the evening, I have spoken to many people who love me and whom I love. They listened to me. They cried and laughed with me. And somehow, with their support, I sent the dark day on its way. "Get out of town," I said. "You're not welcome here."

I look out the window. The storm has passed. The sun shines brighter than I have ever seen it shine. Maybe that's what is so valuable about darkness… the brightness afterward.

—

Giving Thanks

At Thanksgiving, gratitude takes center stage. It lifts its head from obscurity and dominates our plans. "You've forgotten me long enough," it complains as it dusts itself off from constant neglect. "Time to pay me some attention."

But gratitude is so much more; it reminds me of the time I walked with an artist down a street in the midst of winter. She stopped and stared at a barren tree. "What are you looking at?" I asked her, for there were no leaves, just twisted limbs against a gray sky. "Beauty," she answered. "Aren't we lucky to be able to see such a tree?" Twenty years later, I am grateful to own that memory.

Another… a quadriplegic participating in wheelchair sports wins a medal while I watch. He can barely move from the neck down by himself. "It's terrific being able to compete," he tells me during our conversation. "I'm so grateful I could travel here and be part of this."

My six-year-old granddaughter Jenny reads from her first book. I listen with wonder at each word she struggles to pronounce. The thoughts slip from the pages into her mind as I share the experience. "Thank you for this moment," I tell her.

A neighbor brings me a black vase. I had admired it on his porch. He says it belongs on mine. I am grateful, not only for the vase, but for the generosity coming with it.

Slivers of beauty.

Gratitude reminds me there are thousands of moments such as these that I forget to appreciate. A bird sitting on a pole surveying the neighborhood as if it lives there, filling the morning air with its pure song. The sun stirring behind the horizon, bringing a new opportunity to change one's life or to embellish another's. Gratitude reminds me that it is the favor done and the favor received, the loving gesture, the unselfish act, that enables it to survive. The goodness in human beings gives it hope and energy.

There are so many things to be grateful for. Family, friends, health, fulfilling work, discovery, challenges, the sweet touch of the universe as it shelters us. Too many to list or to remember.

I realize I haven't thought about such benefits in a long time. I haven't said, "thank you," to those to whom I am grateful, to those who have given me support, made each day better, joined me in this adventure, committed themselves to my dreams, offered their assistance, shared what they had to give me more, believed in my ability to become wiser, stronger, and survive life's twists and turns.

Today I honor gratitude.
By thanking all of you for being in my life.

—

The Yellow Brick Road

In other times it might have been called a wrong number. I was searching for senior publishing markets on the Internet. Instead, I found senior e-mail clubs. I knew instantly I was in the wrong place. Part of me urged, "Leave right now. This is not what you're looking for."

But another voice coaxed, "Why not investigate? Perhaps destiny played a hand in this. Why not take a trip on the Internet? Why not travel around the world the way you never would in person?" Not knowing much about the computer and less about the e-mail clubs, I let my fingers guide me, filling in one space, and then another, offering some information, holding back what I considered private.

I could choose my pen pal, a male or female, as many as I wished, married, single, in this country or that. Slowly I proceeded, going further into the questionnaire, when suddenly, there appeared before me a list of countries around the world.

I chose my country and several people from it. I wrote them something about myself. Curiosity had dominated. I wondered if anyone would respond to my query. And then I turned off the machine and forgot about it.

Until the next day when, "You have mail," greeted me. Someone had returned my message. And within a day we had traded information about husbands and wives, family and interests, and shared a connection, though miles of ocean separated us. How easily the trust came. No face to interfere. No threat of immediate contact. Just a written word floating across the miles… becoming part of my life. He too was a writer. He too lived near the sea. He too collected sea glass. He had three children, I two. He was happily married, I had been. We both had connected in this fantasy world of the Internet and were stunned that we entered each other's lives so easily, with so much trust, like children playing in the park, without fear of the new playmates following them down the slide.

The letters kept going back and forth. Only a week before, I didn't know him or his family or much about his country, except what I read in the newspapers or watched on television. But now I knew his country from his heart and soul, and his country seemed different already. Now I knew something about his life, his home, his talent. And he knew about me as I spoke of my life in America. Thoughts slipped out so easily with this pen pal, as if they had been waiting for the opportunity.

Do I need another friend, I ask myself as I write another

letter to my Internet friend. Not really. I have many, all loyal, all loving. All eager to give me the time I need from them. Am I missing something in my life, I think as I receive another letter on my computer. I think not. Family is devoted and available, an ocean nearby lends its spirituality, there are men in my life. Everything seems quite in the right place. And yet, the fascination of this new connection, lingers.

I am reminded of the fairy tales I read as a child. A trip to another time and place where no one had an address or a job. All the make-believe characters lived in the middle of somewhere, the place one does not touch or see, the magic place of fantasy. A journey into a story, and I returned satisfied that this other world would not abandon me. Because most of it was in my mind, in my imagination. I didn't have to face the reality of the wicked witch, or the frog who was really a prince, or the beauty who lost her slipper. We were hidden from each other and connected only when we wished, with no schedule, no duty, no assignment. And yet they were my best friends and knew a part of me no one else could reach. It was as if they held a lifeline to a place inside myself too fragile to expose elsewhere. All of my fairy tale creatures cooperated within their cloak of mystery to keep me interested and coming back. They were miles away, across the ocean of make believe, and I was traveling down their Yellow Brick Road toward the Wizard of Oz.

I feel I am again walking down the Yellow Brick Road. Only this time it's called the World Wide Web.

⁓

Grandparenting

BOOK THREE

A Good Laugh

I needed a good laugh, a belly laugh, a deep, right-from-the-gut spontaneous laugh. I needed to shake with laughter, to be in stitches, burst out laughing. I needed to feel it roll up inside me and shoot out, uncontrollably.

I don't laugh enough. Often, I forget I have the gift of laughter. Perhaps I neglect to notice that things are funny. Or that humor deserves to be appreciated. Or that life doesn't always have to be serious.

I laughed a lot when I was younger. For some reason, it just seemed easier to find things to laugh about. I had a friend once who rarely said anything funny and yet when we were together, we would just look at one another and break out in laughter. It didn't matter where we were or what we were doing. Everything seemed hilarious to us. Other people. What they were doing. Even ourselves. We took nothing seriously when we were together. Certainly not life. Life was the biggest joke of all. But in my senior years, I find fewer reasons to invite laughter into my life. Illness, loneliness, frustration, discourage its entrance.

But laughter is not something to be forever ignored or rejected. Its free spirit is stubborn. Nor can it be told the right time to appear. I recall being in a very quiet room during a lecture. The person next to me said something funny. A smile would have sufficed. Instead, I laughed. Just a giggle at first. But each time I looked at the person next to me, the laughter increased in size and sound. I could not contain it, control it, or myself. People turned to look at me. "What kind of person is this?" they must have thought. A serious lecture and there she sits, laughing. Boldly laughing. The more I tried to stop, the more laughter wouldn't let me. It seemed to know I needed it. Desperately. More than I needed to hear the lecture. More than I needed to sit properly, silent. More than I needed to be an adult in control, doing the right thing. That day, more than anything, I needed what laughter had to offer. Later, after wiping my eyes, for hearty laughter can often bring one to tears, I apologized for my behavior to those sitting next to me.

"I just don't know what happened to me," I admitted. Laughter comes and goes that way, without explanation.

Today, I drive my grandson Ryan from my house to his. He tells me a story of something he did in school.

"You didn't!" I say in disbelief.

"I did! I did!" he answers.

"You didn't. You didn't. You didn't." I reply, with a smile.

He picks right up on it. "I did. I did. I did," he giggles, playing the game.

Two blocks pass in silence.

"You didn't!" I surprise him.

Four more blocks go by. "I did." He returns the surprise.

We are laughing. We are laughing, and we don't know why. We go over the bridge. He is giggling, trying to contain himself. I know what he is thinking. We each are anticipating the other's next reply. We are joined together in one thought and laughter is our connection.

"You didn't," I whisper at the other end of the bridge.

"I did," he whispers as we cross the railroad tracks. The laughter ripples through the car. We can't contain it. It warms me. It softens the hard day. It lights up the face looking at me in my car mirror. We want to say more but we can't stop laughing.

We pull up at Ryan's house. He kisses me, opens the door and before he rushes out, shouts, "I did!" I hear his laughter as he opens his front door.

I feel refreshed, as if I have just taken a cool shower, or walked through the spring grass. It is so easy to laugh when you're with the right person.

—

A Grandmother Again

Each time is like the first time. I'm a grandmother again. Ryan was my first grandchild and I thought nothing could surpass the feeling. He expanded my life the moment I felt his finger curl around mine. My world was never the same again. Jenny blew in during a snowstorm, and the moment she set her dark eyes upon mine, I was her prisoner. Jake's smile was in his eyes, and when he opened them during our introduction, I wondered how I could have thought life was complete without his presence. And now my daughter-in-law, Liz has given birth to Ben. I think of him as "Gentle Ben" because, although his cry is gusty, his gaze is thoughtful and I sense a gentleness within his soul. One that I can't wait to share.

I will need time with this new grandchild for we have important moments to fill and life to study. The clouds especially. I have much to say about clouds. I don't think we pay enough attention to the sky. After all, it hangs above us daily, but how many actually look up? I want to look up with Ben and see what we can find up there. Raindrops can be interesting if you try to catch them in your mouth as they fall. Snowflakes can be just as enticing, especially when they turn into a snowman or a sleigh ride. And the wind; we can't forget the wind blowing an autumn leaf from a tree. Perhaps we could follow it down the path. Ben and I have a lot to do together.

Exploring is one of them. Growing things in the summer and chasing worms and ants, and playing with pebbles and dirt. We will find time for all of this, as well as sitting next to one another and just thinking. Or telling stories. Or sharing feelings. Ben and I can do that any time. I'll clear my schedule.

I don't want to rush Ben. But I have so much to share. A big porch with seashells on it. Rocking chairs eager to be filled. A first trip to the ocean. A walk through the sand. Searching for sea glass.

I am not the only one waiting. My animal family waits. I have cats who will purr this baby to sleep and a dog who will wash his face with affection, and a bird who will teach him the beauty of song. Turtles who will teach patience, and fish who will teach serenity. I will show this child how animals love and give and share, taking away loneliness. And when he is old enough, we shall sleep in the big bed together. I will assure this new grandchild when there is a nightmare floating around that the cats and dogs will chase it away.

There are limits to the things I can do. I can't solve eating problems, sleeping problems, potty-training problems, or disciplinary problems, except when they occur on my time and on my property. Instead, I shall concentrate my efforts on the really important matters in life. I shall make sure the outside bird-feeder is filled so Ben and I can watch the birds dine. I will make certain we have a full supply of coloring books and crayons. I shall always set aside time for the urgent business of sucking lollipops and slurping ice cream. And I shall try never to be too busy for a game of marbles, or too rigid to break a rule now and then.

Ben will remind me of the important matters in life, such as smiling and laughing, skipping and crawling, jumping and running, and whispering special secrets to each other. We will explore winding roads and backyard mysteries, and each day will hold a new discovery.

It will be his first time. For everything in this world.

And a first time again, for me.

—

Busy Bees

B oy, am I glad I'm not a kid today. I don't care how many computers they have or television sets or video games. I don't care how many things they've got to keep them busy. I don't care how much money they've got in their pockets, or appointments on their calendars. Or how much education they are getting. They don't know a thing about the free-time zone.

My grandchildren were visiting for the week. They came with a written calendar of events. Pick-up times and drop-off times. My daughter, Beth and her husband, Todd, were traveling abroad. I was in charge of keeping the children busy and on schedule. I'm not good at either. As an elder adult, I manage to keep occupied, but I don't think I'm busy. My dog doesn't care if he's busy. He just wants his walk twice a day. And my cats, in between long naps, avoid being busy. I do not have a busy house, though I have a business in my home.

I wasn't certain how my grandchildren would react to the lack of activity, to the abundance of free time. "What are we doing today?" they would ask. "I don't know," I'd answer. I could see by their faces it was not the expected reply. Somehow we managed to pass the day. We did some staring at the squirrels running up the tree. We took the dog for a walk and played ball with him. We sat on rocking chairs watching people walk up and down the street, and we wondered aloud where they were going. We spent some time talking to the parakeet in his cage, and taking some long walks around the corner and up the block. We drew some chalk pictures on the sidewalk and for an hour or two, we just sat being bored. But that was O.K. Because in the free-time zone, you don't have to be entertaining or exciting or wonderful all the time. Or busy. You can just be.

But kids today are accustomed to being like busy bees. They're busy from the time they get up until the time they go to bed. And it's a long day. Some of them get up at 7:00 a.m. and don't go to bed until 10:00 or 11:00 p.m. Not only are they busy at school, but they are busy with after school activities, and with keeping up with their friends who are also busy. They do a lot of traveling in cars, keeping busy going from one house to another to fulfill playdates. Play is no longer spontaneous. It's scheduled, as are dance classes, soccer and baseball, religious classes and, add to the itinerary, doctor and dentist appointments.

There is little free time. Unscheduled time is a rare treasure, on the brink of becoming extinct. People fear it, run from it, and avoid it. One morning during my weekend in charge of the children, we lay in my king-sized bed all morning deciding what to do with the day. We thought about it a long time. We watched television. We talked. We told each other things we didn't have time to share before. We explored our feelings about the day and about some problems disturbing us. We even dared to be silent with each other. Nobody moved to get dressed. Nobody made a telephone call to a friend. We didn't know what was going on outside the house. We didn't even care. We were in the free-time zone, the no-time zone, the no-clock, no-schedule, no-pressure zone, where it doesn't matter if there's nothing to do. And no place to go.

The free-time zone, where creativity, imagination, and truth roam unconfined, at last.

~

Groovin'

"What do you mean, he has other plans?" I asked my daughter. "He was supposed to visit with me today."

We were talking about my nine-year-old grandson, Ryan. He always jumped at the chance to visit me. We played in the backyard with the dog, Sparky. We talked to the birds, chased the squirrels, worked at my writing desk. Sometimes we just sat next to each other, perfectly comfortable in our silence. On special occasions, we would go out for dinner. Just the two of us. Ryan always ordered double hamburgers with extra pickles. He used a half bottle of ketchup on his french fries.

"He has a playdate," my daughter replied.

I stiffened at the word, "playdate." For some reason, it annoyed me. Play was play. Spontaneous. Unplanned. What was this "date" thing?

I had another reason for my annoyance. There had been many playdates recently. One visit to a classmate after school. Another running with a friend, under a water hose on a hot day. In between there was baseball, basketball, jumping in leaves and exploring assorted mysteries only nine-year-olds could discover. There were dozens of offers for playdates. And very little time for me.

"Where's Ryan?" became the family query.

"Playdate," was the expected response.

Who was that flash racing down the driveway, with a basketball in one hand and a baseball in the other? "Hi grandma," Ryan would say, planting a quick kiss on my cheek as he sped away from the house.

"What about our trucking business," I called to him, though he was out of earshot. When he was younger, Ryan and I spent hours operating our trucking business. We'd line up our plastic trucks, put them in garages, and spend hours traveling from the kitchen to the living room, delivering our goods. Often, after business hours, we drew chalk pictures on the front sidewalk. Ryan didn't seem to enjoy that as much any more. Nor the quiet times. He grew restless. "What else is there to do?" he'd ask. And then when we found something else to do, like a game of Scrabble, just when the game was getting good, the telephone would ring. It would be for him. When he returned to the game, he would look at the Scrabble board as if it were a bowl of hot cereal. He hated hot cereal. He didn't have to tell me where he was headed. "Playdate." Wasn't I his buddy also? Had he forgotten our sleepovers, when he called me a Viking warrior because I slept with the eggbeater on my pillow.

You see, Ryan didn't want the dog jumping on the bed while he was asleep. The dog was afraid of the whirring sound of the eggbeater, so Ryan considered it a weapon of war in which I had outwitted the enemy. But those exciting moments between us did not come as often any more.

One night when he was visiting, a song played on the radio. He sang the words and began to move to its rhythm. I joined him. Dancing in my kitchen was my favorite pastime. We each took a part of the room as we spun around, laughing, clapping our hands, keeping a beat to the rock music.

"You like this music?" Ryan asked, surprised.

"I like all music," I responded.

"You're a good dancer," he said. "Maybe next time you come to my house, we'll do some groovin."

I think we have a "playdate."

~

Jenny's Antique

My six-year-old granddaughter stares at me as if she is seeing me for the first time. "Grandma, you are an antique," she says. "You are old. Antiques are old. You are my antique."

I am not satisfied to let the matter rest there. I take out Webster's Dictionary and read the definition to Jenny. I explain, "An antique is not only old, it's an object existing since, or belonging to, earlier times... a work of art... a piece of furniture. Antiques are treasured," I tell Jenny as I put away the dictionary. "They have to be handled carefully because they sometimes are very valuable."

In order to qualify as an antique, the object has to be at least 100 years old.

"I'm only 67," I remind Jenny.

We look around the house for other antiques, besides me. There is a bureau that was handed down from one aunt to another and finally to our family. "It's very old," I tell Jenny. "I try to keep it polished and I show it off whenever I can. You do that with antiques." When Jenny gets older and understands such things, I might also tell her that whenever I look at the bureau or touch it, I am reminded of the aunt so dear to me who gave me the bureau as a gift. I see her face again, though she is no longer with us. I even hear her voice and recall her smile. I remember myself as a little girl leaning against this antique, listening to one of her stories. The bureau does that for me.

There is a picture on the wall purchased at a garage sale. It is dated 1867. "Now that's an antique," I boast. "Over 100 years old." Of course it is marked up and scratched and not in very good condition. "Sometimes age does that." I tell Jenny. "But the marks are good marks. They show living, being around. That's something to display with pride. In fact, sometimes the more an object shows age, the more valuable it is." It is important that I believe this for my own self-esteem.

Our tour of antiques continues. There is a vase on the floor. It has been in my house for a long time. I'm not certain where it came from, but I didn't buy it new. And then there is the four poster bed, sent to me 40 years ago by an uncle who slept in it for fifty years.

One thing about antiques, I explain to Jenny, is that they usually have a story. They've been in one home and then another, handed down from one family to another, traveling all over the place. They've lasted through years and years. They could have been tossed away, or ignored, or destroyed, or lost. But instead, they survived.

For a moment Jenny looks thoughtful. "I don't have any antiques but you," she says. Then her face brightens. "Could I take you to school for show and tell?"

"Only if I fit into your backpack," I answer.

And then Jenny's antique lifted her up and embraced her in a hug that would last through the years.

~

Purple Toenails

"Are you sad today?" my granddaughter Jenny asks.

"A little," I answer.

"Then I will paint your toenails purple," she says. "That will make you feel better."

Jenny begins her handiwork. I do not tell her why I am sad. A five-year-old would not understand that it is because a mother committed suicide today. Last spring her daughter was shot and paralyzed in a random shooting at Columbine High School. And now I carry her pain, even though my day has been perfect.

I walked along the boardwalk this morning with seagulls hovering overhead, as if just for me. They put on a command performance that I could not resist, cawing into the air, dipping toward me in welcome. Their skyward journey assures me they will return tomorrow, and the tomorrow after that.

Later, when I walked up Jenny's driveway, the leaves, burned with red and yellow, fell at my feet in a display that filled the emptiness that haunted me. I picked a few and saved them to bring to Jenny as gifts. Even the clouds cooperated, moving out of the way of a blue sky. There was not a blemish on the day's face.

At the food market, the cashier and I laughed over mutual frustrations and shared our lives. The postman, the children running from school, all smiled and waved hello, to add to my perfect day.

I checked in with the children. Busy, but O.K. I want it to remain that way forever. I do not want life's trickery to invade their lives, its unpredictability to cause them pain. As their mother, I no longer can protect them from life's violence or the cruelty it can impose.

I do not want this day to end. Tonight while I sleep, will it all change? As it did for the mother of the Columbine student. She remains in my thoughts on this otherwise perfect day.

I look down at my feet. My ten toenails have turned purple.

"Just remember," Jenny says. "If you get them wet, the nail polish will come off."

Not even purple toenails last forever.

～

Reaching Out

Book Four

Beautiful Music

I live close to my neighbors. I can hear them cough in the morning and sneeze when they are sick. I can hear the sounds of laughter and music when they party. I can hear their anger and their arguments. Their schedule of daily challenges floats down their driveway and into mine.

I can hear conversations from way up the block. The words travel quickly in the night. A dog barking. A fight between two cats. A couple declaring their love on the front porch. They become a concert brought to my doorstep.

"It's so noisy," guests often say when they visit. "Doesn't it disturb you?"

I lived in the suburbs for 35 years. The lawns were manicured, the houses separated by large backyards and front yards. Even when sitting in the backyard, there were no sounds. Perhaps a dog now and then or a bird. Privacy was the key factor cherished by the homeowners.

There were fences and tall trees and big bushes. Sometimes I would talk to a neighbor and not even see her from my side. We were proud of our quiet streets. No honking car horns. Perhaps somewhere else, but not in our neighborhood. In fact, most comings and goings of life seemed to happen somewhere else, where we couldn't see them. And that was just fine with us.

We had our friends in the community. Our children had their playmates. Most were among the 350 homes. We were different, yet alike. We understood one another. We had the same goals. And yet, I recall feeling very alone on some days, and very lonely. I was amidst many, but I felt secluded, buried in the stillness.

Now it's different. I'm not certain I understand any of my neighbors. They probably do not understand me. We come from diverse religious beliefs and cultural backgrounds. But that doesn't seem to matter. We have a common goal. We are trying to get through the day. Often, their sounds start me going. Their determination to survive reminds me that survival is possible. Their music, a constant reminder of our oneness, vibrates through my home and energizes it.

"Do I mind the noise?" I am asked.

Growing older, I mind silence more.

~

Different and Yet the Same

At first glance, we had nothing in common but the fact that we were both mothers. We were of different financial incomes, different races, even different ages. She worked full time. The father of her children did not live at home, and the hardness in her eyes told me her life had not been easy.

Our houses were close together. It didn't leave much room for children playing. At first it was the basketball. The net hung from their garage door. To the children of this woman, it was like honey to a bee. One friend brought his basketball and five more friends with him. The basketball banged against the garage door, sometimes six hours a day. I finally had to ask them to confine their playing to a few hours. The eyes looking back at me were not kind. And so my daily complaints began.

There was a baseball game in front of their house, but the ball managed to find its way onto my porch. It hit a potted plant on my railing and broke the pot.

"Do you think you could play farther over your way?" I asked.

They obeyed politely, but I knew from their unhappy faces, they did not understand. Yet, I didn't understand why each day they seemed to be doing something that made my day uncomfortable. I found myself wishing that family hadn't moved next door, then things could be the way they had been before … quiet and serene.

One night, I stood on a small ladder, struggling to change the light bulb in the porch light overhead. It was difficult because the space was small and my fingers too large. I moved the ladder back and forth, trying to get the right balance. I felt eyes in the dark, looking at me. They were the eyes of the mother. For a moment we stood there in the night staring at one another. She observed a 66-year-old woman, ready to give up, allowing a light bulb to take away her desire to survive.

She smiled across the porch, a warm, understanding smile that encouraged me, and at that moment we were one, with everything in common that mattered. I knew she understood what it was like to be alone and to have to do everything for and by yourself. She knew what it was like to make all the decisions, to curse a light bulb because it wouldn't fit into place.

Tomorrow, I shall buy a large bag of lollipops to give to her children. I will enjoy their laughter and their energy. I will offer my friendship instead of my impatience.

And if a porch pot happens to get broken by a flying baseball, I'll just get another pot.

Hometown, U.S.A.

I want to live in Hometown, U.S.A. I want to pack my bags and move there tomorrow. I know they'll want me even though I'm old. I know they'll want me even though I have little money in my pockets. I know they'll want me with my imperfections. I know they'll understand my needs.

I am searching for my Hometown, U.S.A. I know what it will look like. It will have tree-lined streets with houses, big backyards, and also some apartments. But then again, it might not. It could have dwellings of all sizes and shapes, painted assorted colors. Yet, in my eyes, each will have beauty. All types of people will live out their lives in Hometown U.S.A. Some will like each other, some will not. Some will think each other strange because they have nothing in common. But in Hometown, U.S.A. it wouldn't matter because there is a bountiful supply of understanding. Enough to go around for everybody. Enough to last a lifetime.

There would be a Main Street in Hometown, U.S.A. Everything I would need would be there. I could shop for food, go to the dentist, get my hair cut, eat at a restaurant, visit the park, stop at the hardware store. There would be no need to take a car if I wished to walk. Main Street would stretch across the town, reaching out to everywhere.

Everyone would feel welcome in my Hometown U.S.A. For everyone would have something to offer. I, as an older adult, would have living experience and the ability to survive, and the youngsters and those in between would 'do the doing' that has to be done. We would all be connected in Hometown, U.S.A., and each problem and each crisis would be shared. Hometown U.S.A. would believe in sharing.

Nobody would feel alone. A best friend could be a neighbor or someone at the community center. In this Hometown U.S.A. best friends could include the policeman who knows everybody in the town, the fireman who risks his life for those he sees each day on the street, the grocer who greets everyone, and the doctor who knows their body histories. No one would be without a best friend. And neighbors would have time to talk with one another. They would talk over back fences and on sidewalks and in driveways. They would ask each other, "How you doin?" and care about the answer.

My Hometown, U.S.A. would be a caring town. It would care about its stray cats and dogs, about its streets and sidewalks, about its backyards and front yards, about its buildings, and about the people who work in the buildings. It would care about those who suffer, those who need, and those who do not know where to take their anger. Everyone would feel loved by somebody in Hometown U.S.A.

This is a town that wouldn't be afraid of the word "different." There would be people of different languages and different colors and different backgrounds and different faiths. And different visions. But this wouldn't frighten Hometown U.S.A. It would only strengthen it.

I know Hometown, U.S.A. is waiting for me to arrive. We are eager to find one another. Any day now, I feel it's about to happen.

—

I Bought an American Flag Today

I bought an American flag today. I am ashamed to say I didn't own one. Somewhere along the way, I had forgotten some very important things about that flag. I remember having a flag once… was it in the attic… or had it been put away in a box in the basement? Somehow it had disappeared.

I didn't miss it for many years. I noticed it hanging in other places. I glimpsed at it in magazines and on television. I caught the colors of its cloth in front of parks, and schools and in parades.

But somehow the flag had disappeared from my life, and from the house I lived in. Quietly. It didn't protest as holidays passed by, as wars began and ended, as new Presidents were sworn in.

As a child, whenever the flag appeared on television, I was told to stand. Even at other people's houses. "Stand, Harriet," one of my parents ordered. "It is our flag." Others in the room stood with us. I remember my shoulders straightening, my head lifting with pride.

Somehow, I had forgotten to tell my children, my grand-children how I felt about our flag.

I bought an America flag today. Some who watched me purchase it and carry it out of the store, who watched me place it in the bracket attached to my house, asked me - why? It wasn't a holiday. It wasn't a special day. The flag, which certainly belonged there more than anywhere else in the community, seemed to need a reason for existing in the front of my house, waving its brilliant colors for all to see.

It had a reason. It took the Revolutionary War of Independence to create this great country called America. It took men who surrendered their futures to carry the American flag to victory. It took heroes who gave their lives and asked only for freedom for others in return.

America asked everything from those who pioneered her land and kept her promises alive. She expected sacrifice and commitment. A man had to choose between his country and his family, his country and his work, his country and his life. He chose his country, for his country meant freedom.

I bought an American flag today. And I am grateful that flags do not hold grudges, that it has forgiven that I had forgotten, that it has understood that sometimes I did not understand, that it had the patience when I didn't have the belief, that it didn't turn away from me, when I, during moments of frustration, turned away from it, and that it waited, until I remembered just what a flag can do for a home, for the people in my home, for the block, for the community around my block, and for my town.

I bought an American flag today. And boy, did it feel great. And yes, I had a reason. I bought it because I needed to re-member the men and women who fought for this great na-tion, and died for it; for those missing-in-action and for hostages not returned. I bought the flag because I had to have something that would show my love for my country.

Nothing could show it better.

—

The Wall

It was a sunny day at the beach. They were young children. Different races. Different backgrounds. Different lifestyles. They didn't know each other before that afternoon. Not until they became involved with the Wall.

Somewhere out at sea, a storm gathered. The waves tossed high, gaining power. Too treacherous for swimming. Beach-goers were allowed at the water's edge, but no farther. Children were cautioned to stay out of the dangerous currents that could pull at their small feet and young bodies and drag them into deeper waters.

One of the children began to build a sand wall. It was his intention to keep this mighty ocean away from the castle he had built. After all, he had worked on it all afternoon and now it was being threatened by an ocean out of control. So he began working on his wall. He had very small hands and very heavy sand to carry back and forth to the wall in front of his castle. He rushed across the beach, up and down to the water's edge, bringing his supply of wet sand that would fortify his protective wall. For those who watched, it was clear that it was a futile enterprise that would take much longer than one person could possibly manage in a day. His castle could not survive for many more minutes with the storm headed in its direction.

Another child standing nearby, sensed the emergency, and decided to help. The two began working together, carrying, lifting, pounding, racing against the incoming tide. A third boy who had been watching the two, joined with them, piling the wet sand on the wall, mixing it with dry sand, making it stronger. A few girls passing by surveyed the castle, the growing wall, which was now widening as many feet as there were children, and they joined in the construction. In a short time, the wall grew higher. And wider.

The working crew also expanded. More children were attracted to the wall and to the battle to preserve the castle. Even though it wasn't their castle. Even though they had never been introduced to each other. Though they were strangers to one another, they had a common goal. To hold back the ocean. Adults might have advised their mission was impossible. But to younger minds, it became the irresistible challenge.

The children laughed with one another as they piled the sand higher and gave each other instructions. There were discussions as to how high the wall should be and how thick, and which sand was the best, the wet or the dry, and how much time they had to complete their task. The waves refused to accept defeat as they beat against the barricade, adding cracks as quickly as they were mended, taking sand away as quickly as it was added.

Now it became a battle of wits and endurance between the sand-gatherers and the changing tide. The wall symbolized something that only the children involved could understand. Parents called to them that it was time to go home. "In a minute," one answered. "Not yet," said another. Their faces took on determination. They had worked too hard and too long to give up now. Even though the white caps taunted them, slapping their construction around roughly, the wall held strong. Each time a wave failed to diminish its exterior, the group (and it had become a group by now) shouted in victory.

Again and again, without mercy, the waves pounded, but the wall stood firm. The children formed tunnels, decorated it with seashells, added buckets filled with sand to fortify it, sang songs in front of it, and dared the ocean to destroy what they had built.

Eventually the children went their separate ways. But the wall remained upright for hours, protecting the castle. Even curious adults were amazed at its endurance. It had come to represent much more than a pile of sand. Many children had joined together, and in that moment on the beach, the impossible became possible.

Walls sometimes separate. This one didn't.

~

Relationships

BOOK FIVE

Being Needed

We read a lot about Baby Boomers needing to take care of their parents, either in their own homes or in nursing homes. Age, illness, and just the scars of living take their toll. Children at some age must think about taking care of their parents.

But about parents taking care of their children? Even at a later age. Even when children are in their middle years, even when they should be independent, needing nothing but their own decision-making powers. Even when all the teaching and bringing up, and scolding and ordering, and guiding are over. What could be left for parents to do? Many my age long to be selfish for once in their lives, to be rid of the every day needs and responsibilities of their children. "It's time for us now," they say.

I find that my job as a mother is not over yet. In today's world of technology, of both parents often working, of a hectic pace, of the stress of measuring up and keeping up with the expectations of those around them, my services are needed more than ever. Those motherly skills I thought would be un-called for, unneeded, packed away at this time in my life, are now being used in a different way. Not only for my grandchildren. But for my children, as well.

My supply of motherly gifts is not unwanted or ignored. They are offered indirectly, subtly. From wherever I am, they are delivered without payment due. "I am still learning too, " I tell my children, eager to share my discoveries. When I was ill, I fought to regain my health. Sometimes I wanted to give up, but I knew my children were watching. My choices would either teach them how easily it would be to surrender, or how to fight back and survive. I felt them waiting. My motherly instincts surfaced and I fought as never before. "See," my actions told them. "This is what it is like to be down and out and yet not quite out." And I felt their admiration as I struggled.

Sometimes it is not that complex. It is simplicity that wins center stage. The family will gather for dinner on my porch. Someone will joke about my poor cooking. Another family member will run out to pick up spaghetti sauce for which I boil enough spaghetti for twice the number of people expected. Some things will never change. But I am the keeper of tradition, and memories, and things only a mother knows. And, I am needed to guard their past, applaud their present, and give them faith in their future.

There are many things I do not know about my children.

And probably never will. They are entitled to privacy and their own mistakes. They are entitled to the stories they share only with friends or husbands and wives. But now and then there is a reaching out, a desperate call, a need beyond what they have. No matter how old, no matter how successful, no matter how sophisticated they become. They dial my number.

That's when I'm grateful to be here.

—

Emancipated Lady

I knew a woman who was into a relationship with a man. Both were single. He wanted her to hold his hand whenever they walked together. He also wanted her to sleep with him. He said today's woman understood such expectations. He wanted a full relationship. Without living with her. Without supporting her through life. Without marriage. After all, he said, she was a liberated woman.

I knew another woman who, through much of her fifty years of marriage, sat alone on weekends while her husband ran his business in his house, seven days a week. She kept herself busy with volunteer work, but inside, she festered. And yet she spoke of herself as a liberated woman.

Another woman who thought herself emancipated, flew to her lover every few months. There were no promises, no commitments other than their immediate enjoyment. She prided herself on her liberation, on her flexibility, and yet, when he found another woman, and without much sensitivity, told her of his new love, she was devastated.

A psychologist friend and I often get into long conversations about the emancipated woman and her relationships with men. I tell him constantly that I am liberated in every way, have been so for years and yet often, I see myself doing something or saying something that shows my vulnerability and dependency. "Being emancipated isn't all it's cracked up to be," I tell my old friend. "Sometimes I just want to lean on a man and let him do the steering, even if it's not where I want to go. Can't I just do that now and then?" But I realize even before he answers, I would have no control over my destination. And no right to complain of the outcome.

"If you're giving away your dignity and your self-respect just to feel safe, and if you grow not to like yourself with the partner you've picked, whatever your living conditions, don't call yourself an emancipated lady," my good friend says. "You have to be comfortable with a man. If he makes you uncomfortable by his demands and you stay with him; if you feel inside that it's wrong for you and you continue the relationship, then you're giving up your freedom, your dignity and everything that goes with it."

I told him it's not easy to be alone and emancipated. There always seems to be a good reason to hold onto whatever you've got, even if there are disappointments, compromises, disillusionment, and the battering of dignity and self-respect. Nobody is perfect, right? People hurt each other, right? They say they're sorry, right? Isn't that the way it works? I tell him I do just fine at work or with friends, but in a relationship with a man, I slip back into the role of always pleasing. "It's important that I make him happy," I say. I really don't know where I got that part of the story. It just seems that is the way it is. If he is happy, I am happy.

"That's O.K.," my psychologist friend says, "as long as you're honest with yourself. But don't call yourself an emancipated lady. Someone has the controls and it's not you. And, what about your happiness?"

"But isn't that being selfish?" I reply.

"An emancipated lady wouldn't even ask that question," he responds.

I guess I have more work to do on myself to earn that title.

—

Feelings

We sit around chatting. We are in our sixties, seventies, eighties. One woman is 85. She admits, "I have emotional needs that aren't being met. I want to tell my children what I am feeling, but I can't seem to do it," she tells us. She needs a phone call once a week. She needs to connect with them. She needs a visit now and then, or to go to their houses for dinner occasionally. She needs to sit in their homes and feel the activity. She needs to belong to family. She needs to be part of her children's lives. Not every day. "I want them to help me. There are medical papers and decisions. I don't know how I wound up so alone. I don't know why I have to be totally independent and not need them." She has three grown children living nearby. She says they are good children, with very active lives.

Another shares her story. She is 80. "I'm working on a more positive feeling about myself. Acceptance. Not being negative." She tells us that she is taking care of herself and trying not to worry about anyone else. There is no energy for others. She has her everyday needs. She drives herself to her doctor, shopping, banking, to the movies. She admits to being angry at times, disappointed in life, disappointed in herself. So she works on her feelings. She reads books. She thinks a lot about her attitude. Her goals... a positive attitude and independence.

Enjoying solitude is sought after by another. He tells us that he was afraid to be alone after his wife died. A man working outside his home his entire life, he found himself alone inside. He couldn't handle it, so he rushed into the outside world to keep himself busy. He dated, joined groups, attended classes, filled his life up, and thought he was content. Except he hadn't really faced the initial problem; being alone inside the house. Now he has decided to do that, to enjoy his solitude. He tells us that he has learned through reading and talking to others that solitude doesn't necessarily have to be lonely. That it can be enriching also. When he is alone inside his house and listens to music, he says he really listens now. With all his senses. He feels the music inside him. And when he eats alone, he does so with a new attitude. He sets the table carefully for an important person who is coming to dine. Himself. And even when he goes outside now, he doesn't immediately reach out for company. He can walk alone and enjoy it. He observes more, thinks more. He says it has taken work to enjoy his solitude and to use it differently.

The conversation deepens. Though we do not know each other that well, each of us shares. It is age that brings us together and it is age that brings trust amongst us. There are experiences we don't have to explain because each of us has been there. But what we find important during this discussion is that we can express our feelings and be understood. The same feelings we often hid and protected, the feelings that sometimes embarrassed us or made us feel weak; we now surrender to each other.

"I feel so young inside some days," a man tells us. He is 75. "Like a young boy," he smiles. "Like seventeen. If I didn't look in the mirror, I would think I was 17. But what is the sense of feeling that way if nobody around you sees you that way." We tell him it doesn't matter about others. We see him that way.

The media tells us we are becoming a graying America. There will be more of us. A group of writers in Hollywood is suing because they can't get work. Age discrimination, they say. They are 50 and over. They say the business considers them finished, that they have nothing to offer the young audience. They don't feel finished. Their list of accomplishments is long and commendable. But that doesn't seem to matter. So they are fighting back.

In our circle of talk, our feelings are out on the table where we can see them. We help the 85-year-old woman prepare her dialogue with her three sons so that she can tell them what she needs. It will take courage to unveil herself, to let them see her as she is. She will talk about her feelings.

We are fighting back also.

Feeling Whole

Awoman told me her story. She was married 43 years when her husband passed away. They were happy together. And then he was gone. "I no longer felt whole," she told me. And that's the way it was for over two years; feeling as if half of her had vanished. Wherever she went, she felt incomplete. Not enough. Half empty. Always, she looked at other couples and envied their togetherness.

But it was the loneliness she talked about, that she remembered. Devastating loneliness. After having someone for so long, she couldn't face the haunting days that awaited her every morning and every night when she went to bed, alone. She volunteered in her community, took some courses, joined some groups, had supportive friends, and loving children. But it was a partner she needed and wanted. Nothing else could replace what she had lost.

And then she met a man. Very much unlike her husband. Very troubled. Very controlling. Very argumentative. With two marriages behind him. Estranged from his family. From friends. In every way, unlike her mate of 43 years.

And yet, he was so appealing, attractive, and loving toward her. He was romantic, and made her feel as if she were seventeen again. They ate picnic lunches, went to the movies and enjoyed breaking the rules. They sat on the beach at night, huddled in blankets, and felt the giddiness of youth. They spent days and evenings wrapped in each other's arms. "I was a girl again," she said. After 43 years in a marriage, the girl sometimes becomes a tired woman. This man brought her to life.

And so their year together continued. A break-up, then reconciliation, as she fled each time from loneliness into his embrace. It was a difficult relationship, the price for his companionship, high. It drained her, and yet . . .

"It was so wonderful when it was good," she recalls.

And then he died. Suddenly. And after she buried him, she told me she didn't feel complete any longer. Again, she felt half a person. The half remaining was distraught and empty, more insecure and frightened than ever before. She was back where she started when her husband had passed away. She couldn't bear that feeling. So the search began for another man. "I know I'll find him," she said. "And then I'll feel whole again."

Today I watched a sunrise spill across the ocean.

And I felt whole.

—

Sixteen Again

I am sixteen again. I didn't think I would return to this age. I thought it was gone forever. Certainly when I am three years away from being 70. But it has returned. I am dating. Just as I did when I was sixteen.

And I find I am just as uncertain, foolish, and determined to be free. How can that be? I find myself primping before a date. Should I wear this or that? Did I wear it last week? Where will we go? What will we talk about? I become nervous, lose my self-confidence, and wonder why I am doing this to myself. Entering the single dating world, the one I hated so much when I was sixteen.

I am sixteen again, just as uncertain, just as untrained. After 35 years of marriage, this widow emerges as a liberated woman who hasn't the slightest idea what to do with her liberation. At sixteen, the first time around, all I cared about was polishing my fingernails, listening to dreamy music, and wondering who would come into my life the next day or the next week. Nothing has changed.

Just as when I was sixteen, there were the two dreaded statements that sent me fleeing. One was, "You sure you're not frigid? Everyone does it unless they're frigid." The other, "Let's go steady." I find being that age again, nothing has changed. I still run in the opposite direction. The words might be more grown-up, but the meaning has remained the same.

I have no sense about dating. As I didn't then. There were many boys walking through the doorway, so many in fact, that my mother constantly got their names mixed up. "Just don't call them anything," I pleaded as she said hello to Ed who was Lenny and Lenny who was Paul. I changed dates as I would clothes. Why not. Sixteen wouldn't come around again.

But it did. At 67. And here I am wanting to change clothes as I did then. I am repeating old habits. Perfume bottles that haven't been opened for too long, are now half empty. Nail polish is one of my necessities when I shop. Stockings certainly can't have runs in them and my make-up supply never runs out. I am playing dreamy music and dancing in my kitchen. Sometimes alone. Sometimes not. I talk on the telephone with single women friends and we discuss guys, endlessly. As I did before.

I didn't expect to approach my seventh decade in this teenage state. As a mother, grandmother, cancer survivor, widow, I am now carrying baggage that might discourage a suitor. White hair, lined face, a figure that has taken a beating.

My inventory certainly has depleted. And yet life has offered me other assets. A smile that refuses to dim, the ability to listen, and a certain contentment about who I was and who I am. And since younger men call me "foxy," perhaps my inventory is sufficient.

I do not go out to search as I did when I was sixteen, at dances, or on blind dates. This time around, men just drop into my life. And remain. My mother's favorite saying was, "Faint heart never won fair maiden." I keep that in mind on date-night. And that's another thing that is the same. What to do on a Saturday night. Or even Friday. I didn't think about those evenings as unusual events when I was married, but now, again, they have become quite important. Significant. Like V-DAY. A celebration.

I have kept my mother's advice about date night well in mind. "Here's some money," she would say. "If any boy does something you don't like, just leave him and make a call home. We'll come get you."

Well, my parents aren't here now, but I've got that money in my pocketbook. Once I was with a man who said something I didn't like. I had taken my car so the rules had changed. This time I told him to get out and walk. And he did.

Sixteen, the second time around, is much more fun.

~

The Right One

Very often people approach me to tell their stories. Each one is unique, and yet often with a similar thread running through it. Loneliness. The loss of a partner. The fear of facing life without companionship.

Just as often, the storytellers are searching for Mr. or Mrs. Right. Not necessarily to marry. Not necessarily to share a commitment or a dwelling. Usually to have a friendship, a male or female partner to trust, to dine with, to laugh with, one who understands without judgment, one who accepts without criticism.

Those who have lost their partners often seek kindness, for they are wounded. And many are still healing.

But as each story substantiates, the partnership has to be right. Using the correct judgment in such matters can be a tricky business. Some talk of second marriages when first ones soured, and the second ones are spurred by loneliness and need, rather than having found the right person.

But learning to know someone takes patience, and waiting

can be difficult when there is no partner to share the beauty of a sunset or the pile of bills that need to be paid.

Some persevere through relationships that are wrong from the beginning, almost as if each wears a large sign on their forehead: "Do not even try to make this right." And yet they try. Because he or she needs the companion to quiet the inner voice that pleads, "Don't make me go through this journey of life alone."

So my storytellers compensate and compromise. They convince themselves they do not deserve better. They persuade themselves that tomorrow things will be better. They tell themselves that it's worth it. They do not have faith in their own singleness, in their oneness, in their own completeness.

They don't recognize or appreciate the friendship, the partnership, the loyalty or the courage coming from themselves. They fear the alternative called loneliness, and think that even a wrong partner is better than none.

And they never discover the power from within.

~

Self Discovery

BOOK SIX

A Senior Moment

"I didn't expect to hear from you today," I tell a friend who is telephoning long distance. She always calls on Friday morning. I think today is Saturday. It is not.

I woke up thinking it was Saturday. I do not know what gave me that impression. I do know yesterday was Thursday and Friday always follows Thursday. In this unpredictable world, that much I know. But this week, I jumped from Thursday to Saturday. I bought the morning paper and circled the garage sales as I do each Saturday morning. I didn't miss Friday nor did I realize it was waiting for me, as it usually does, immediately after Thursday.

"You're having a senior moment," my 55-year-old friend informed me during our conversation. She then confided that several days ago, she had shown up at work on Monday, ready to start her week. Only it was Sunday and the office was closed.

My animals look forward to my senior moments. Sometimes I forget that I fed them once, and I feed them twice.

As long as I'm confessing, I might as well tell of the time I lost my eyeglasses somewhere in the house and found them in the refrigerator. I think when I went for a bottle of soda, I left the eyeglasses as a deposit. On the upside, it was a hot day and I found wearing them cold and refreshing.

I have found that senior moments are also familiar to people under 50. Often, when I am visiting my daughter's house, my grandson, Ryan, will ask, usually moments before the school bus is to arrive, "Did anyone see my other shoe?" And my granddaughter, Jenny, is usually frantically running around looking for her school bag. Ryan is 10. Jenny is 6.

My daughter who is 42 years old, put her pocketbook on the trunk of her car one day and forgot to take it off. We took a long ride, followed by some young teenagers, who delighted in watching the pocketbook bump up and down. Their honesty prevailed when we drove over the railroad tracks, and the bag dropped to the ground. They retrieved and returned it. "What was it doing on the railroad track?" my daughter asked them. "You had a senior moment," I wanted to explain.

My son-in-law, Todd, also 42, usually misplaces his wallet. And no one in the house can ever find the battery-operated telephone. Or the remote control for the TV.

Each day I give myself a short test just to make certain that my memory is still cooperating. I count from 100 backwards to 1, repeat the alphabet from Z to A, and sing several favorite songs, gaining self- confidence as I remember each word. I also try to put everything in the same place I put it the day before. Although sometimes I forget where I put it the day before.

I have a 70-year-old friend who uses crossword puzzles to exercise his mind. Now and then he forgets my name. Shortly after such an incident, I see him frantically working on a puzzle.

I admit to feeling relieved when my son, who is 38, can't find his car keys. Once he had to get a locksmith to unlock his car.

This reassures me. Senior moments are not exclusive.

~

A Wife

I didn't fully appreciate the meaning of the word "wife" when I was married. Now, at this time in my life, as a widow, I truly believe I shall never be called by that name again.

"I'll get my wife for you," a husband responded, when I called on the telephone to speak to a friend. How many times did my husband say those words in 35 years of marriage?

"I'm Eph's wife," I'd respond eagerly, when newly married. I couldn't wait to identify myself with the new title.

But as the years wore on, I didn't think about it as much nor did I appreciate its durability. It became like an old pair of shoes I wore everyday. Comfortable but unnoticed.

Now that I no longer enjoy its comfort, its security, its protection, I notice it all the time. That word called, "wife."

When I became a wife, I took it quite seriously. It was a building, sharing kind of thing. We had dated for awhile, became engaged, and then the loving led to what we thought was the satisfactory conclusion. Marriage. I would become his wife. And he would become my husband. We would begin together.

Being a wife meant many things to me. Sometimes it was wondrous. Children made it so. Family made it so. Knowing each of us had gone the distance for one another, made it so. Taking the final risk. Putting aside doubts, insecurities, and selfishness. Other times it was frightening. A wife forever? Was there something I was missing? Would I or could I have been more without wifehood? And during my angry times or confused times, it became unwanted. Now and then, I just didn't think I needed that title anymore. Many women out there were single, talking about finding themselves, not needing a man, being totally self-sufficient.

But one doesn't shed wifehood without some serious thought. As I grew older and grew up, I found I could be what I wanted to be, feel what I wanted to feel, and miss nothing that would encourage my growth as a human being, all the while continuing to be Eph's wife. I discovered being a wife enhanced my courage and my creativity. Wifehood constantly surprised me, challenging me to wear its cloak of commitment.

Women today feel differently about the word, "wife." We often talk about the "no commitment" relationships. People are living alone or with family, seeing their partner on weekends or on whatever terms they agree. Some even live beneath the same roof and share the expenses. They meet one another's families. They offer each other physical love. But they do not marry. She is never called "a wife."

A woman tells me she has lost her partner. They had gone together for many years.

"It was just like we were married," she says.

Not really, I think.

Not until you want to hear yourself called "wife" do you understand.

~

Mutiny

As I grow older, my body parts become more insistent. They refuse to allow me to forget them. We are in constant arbitration. "Remember us!" they order. "Just do not take us for granted as you did when you were young. Those days are forever gone."

My neck reminds me all the time that it is there. When younger, it was merely an attachment to keep my head in the right place, although sometimes, I must admit my head managed to run off and get lost. However, most of the time, the neck did its job. But now it is cranky, and though it carries my head every day as it must, it certainly protests all the way. Stiff it is. Painful it becomes. "Ouch," I complain as I move this way and that. "Doing the same job for all these years isn't a piece of cake," it answers me. So I exercise it, put warm compresses on it, and gradually, the neck behaves. Until the next time.

My eyes remind me in another way. "Cataracts," the eye doctor says, peering into them. "Nothing to worry about. For now." I spent many hours in the sun as a youngster. I don't remember needing sunglasses then. And in the evening, as an adult, when I drove my car, my eyes behaved and led me where I had to go. Not any more. They insist on sunglasses whenever it is bright outside, and refuse to take me driving anywhere at night. "Are you kidding," they tell me. "We close down at sunset for this kind of travel." Then to make matters worse, they demand shorter hours and better working conditions.

The rest of my body feels the same way. My fingers tingle if I work too long at the computer. And my legs. They certainly can kick up a storm if I don't take our daily walk and instead, sit too long. "You mean we have to move?" they ask in the morning as if they have never moved before. "And bend?" As if it is a new occurrence. "We were much more comfortable lying in the bed, stretched out. You are not going to do that again to us, are you?" They are referring to T'ai Chi. One half hour every morning. They went along with the walking begrudgingly, but T'ai Chi sent them over the edge into mutiny. Just after one session, my legs refused to budge and had the nerve to send pains shooting up one leg and down another. "Try that again," they said, "and you'll see what else we have in store for you." Just like spoiled children. Well, I certainly couldn't let them get away with it, so now every morning we have an ongoing battle. T'ai Chi has been winning, but not without a few warm baths to pacify the rebelling legs.

There are miscellaneous annoyances from body parts that get tired, bored, or obstinate. A hip gives a twinge, the toes let me know there are ten of them, the knees send their own messages even without the legs, and the teeth are abandoning ship at a time when I need them most. Each day, I get out of bed wondering which of my body parts will complain, and which will behave.

I won't get into the internal body parts that have managed to slow down or speed up without my permission, who wake me in the night and disturb my sleep, who refuse to keep a schedule and sometimes have lost all sense of control. They constantly remind me that I have to treat them with tender care or else there is total rebellion. I have learned that certain foods, certain liquids, and certain sleeping habits pacify them, but not for long. My body parts keep me quite busy at this age. But I have warned them that I have no intention of slowing down, or allowing their shifting moods to control me.

I told them they had better be prepared for hard work and good performance on the job. And to remember, "I'm the boss."

Attitude is everything.

—

Redefining Oneself

R ecently, with the death of one of my dearest friends, I ceased being a sister-in-law. At 67, I now find myself without many of the roles that brought me safety and comfort. I am no longer a wife. No longer a mother in the active sense. No children needing to be fed, clothed, taught, nurtured. And now, no longer a sister-in-law. It's as if little by little, my protective covering has been ripped from me, leaving me feeling naked, vulnerable and lost. Without a hat to call my own.

Someone asked me, "Who are you now?" I thought I knew until the question hit me in the face. More important was the next query. "Who do you want to be?"

I have many choices today as a woman living in this 21st century, while so many women before me were limited. They washed their clothes on the rocks, couldn't vote, and died young from childbirth. They were purchased, sold, enslaved, and abused. Not all of them. Not all the time. But as women, they were second class citizens. In some countries, they did not even have the privilege of life after birth. A newborn girl was dumped into the river and her dreams and possibilities were destroyed before she even had a chance. Just because she was a female.

I face none of these disasters. I can look at my peers and see them as senators and congresswomen. I can find them in colleges and in the work place in administrative positions. I can watch them taking care of families, holding down jobs, making independent decisions, running single households. They are not afraid to drop one identity for another, to redefine themselves as many times as necessary. If they put on a hat and it doesn't fit, they buy another, they try another. They are not frightened to throw the old one away and say, "This hat doesn't work for me. But another might. Another will."

At 67, I must learn from them and do the same. Who do I want to be today? What do I want to wear? When one is young, there is less fear to change, less uncertainty when walking down a new road. At my age, the old roads are comfortable. I am frustrated that my challenging days are not over. And, I have discovered that half a century of living doesn't guarantee me contentment or the certainty that I am where I should be. I have the same doubts I had as a teenager, when I wondered what the future might hold.

Around me everywhere are women in their sixties, swapping hats. Some have become world travelers. Others are exploring new occupations. Many are becoming full-time grandmothers, baby-sitting for working mothers. And then there are those bathed in romance, who choose to dance the night away in silver slippers.

Now I'm shopping for a new hat to wear. The only certainty I have is that it will be like nothing I have worn before. It might be bright red with a flower shooting up from it, surprising everyone with its buoyancy. It might be yellow and wide with a brim. It might be dark and mysterious and come over my eyes, causing others to wonder what is hidden beneath it.

But whatever hat I wear, it will be mine.

—

Sexually Alive

Recently, I read a magazine article about sex and seniors. It was by a doctor and it encouraged those in their later years, well into their eighties, to enjoy sex and everything it offers. Many older people inside, and outside of marriage, are doing just that. Perhaps mine is the first older generation to be told it has the ability and the right to be sexually active, and we are now making the same decisions we once made at sixteen, only this time we are liberated ladies.

I don't mind telling you, as a 67-year-old widow, these aren't easy decisions. It's wonderful being a mother and grandmother, it's delightful having friends, it's sublime reading a book, but there's nothing like facing the sexual hunger in a man's eyes when you walk into a room. I am sexually alive and quite proud of it.

And yet being sexually alive doesn't necessarily mean being sexually active. I like to think my sexual aliveness will hang around for a long time. I enjoy feeling a man's body close to mine when we dance, smell his cologne, and feel the touch of his hand on mine. I can dance in my kitchen to romantic music and dream of my knight. There is always a knight, isn't there? He is somewhere in the distance and perhaps we will meet some day. Or maybe we have met already and I don't recognize him yet. And just maybe he's already in my life, waiting.

I am sexually alive but not sexually active. Since my husband passed away, I was forced to make some decisions about my life. Did I want to marry again? Not necessarily. Did I want to live with someone? Not positively. Did I want to be monogamous with a male partner again? Only without a sexual involvement, I decided. After all, if I am taking care of my own life, my bills, and my health, why would I want to assume the sexual responsibility of a man?

And yet it would be so nice to have a partner I could depend on, come home to, lean on when necessary. The tug of old-time habits makes me uncomfortable in my new role. I long for the comfort of a mate. But that takes an energy, a sacrifice I am not willing to make again at this time in my life. My independence, carved deeply during these six years of singlehood, would be reluctant to cooperate.

However, once I'm sexually active without marriage, once I drop the values I believe are essential to my well being and dignity, I won't have to worry about a value system or being tied to one man. Why not explore sexuality in my sixties?

Why stop with just one partner? Why should I promise loyalty and commitment, and a oneness for the title, "girlfriend," when I held the honored title of wife for 35 years. Faithfulness to a relationship without the courage to make a life-time vow seems contradictory.

And yet, what would I feel like after a man and I enjoyed the physical side of love and then he put his jacket on, smiled with satisfaction, and went home? To his world. To his life. What would I feel like when he wasn't there during illness, unexpected sadness or just the quiet times when one needs to look across the room and feel loved?

Many of us single in these later years, who are being told we might have another 20 sexually active years left, are not certain exactly what we are supposed to do about that. Are we abnormal if we abstain? Are we foolish to ignore this sexual freedom? Should we or shouldn't we? Dare we or dare we not? Our children are grown, living their own lives. Does it matter to them what we do with ours? Isn't this our time to live as we please? Isn't it myself I must please most of all? It has taken 67 years to create the fabric that protects my survival. Whatever I add to its design must strengthen its durability.

Some unmarried women my age opt for dining out, movies, cruises, and sex. They say they are happy when the man leaves and are content with their own privacy. Some have live-in situations without marriage. For one reason or another, they do not want a legal permanency to it. Others consider that part of their lives over. The door is shut and they are content with women friends, social gatherings and family. And even others, such as myself, are tuned into the messages in a man's eyes and from his heart, yet feel that acting upon it might weaken a structure that has taken years to create.

For me, the risk is too great, and the price too high.

But at least this time around, I have options.

~

Young Again

I feel so young today. I awoke this way. My body cooperates. It springs out of bed. There are no aches or creaks this morning.

I open the curtain, pull up the shades. I want to shout out the window, "I feel so young today."

I look in the mirror and smile. A young girl smiles back. Her blue eyes are clear, filled with expectation. There is a natural glow to the cheeks.

I dress in something bright, brush my hair one hundred times, put a bow in it. Am I too old at 65 for such an adornment? Not today, for today I am young.

I drive to the bakery to buy some treats for my daughter, for the grandchildren. I will visit them in this splendid mood. One white icing cupcake for Ryan. Two chocolate icing cupcakes for Jenny and Beth. A glazed donut for Todd. I buy myself a cherry Danish. I want to tell the clerk, "I feel so young today."

It's easy to feel young when playing with my grandchildren. A good game of pick-up sticks, building blocks, and considerable time blowing bubbles adds to my youthful day.

Later everything glistens when I leave their playroom and reach the boardwalk. I lean over the railing and gaze at the ocean. I am a young girl today. I can tell the ocean my dreams again, for I have dreams. I can close my eyes and imagine sweet things, romantic things, exciting things. I haven't been able to do that for a long time. I didn't think I would ever do it again. But it's back, the wonder, the magic, the mystery. I am young again and eager to learn, to grow, to change, to dare.

My feet move down the boardwalk, first slowly, then faster and faster until I am running.

Toward a wonderful day.

—

Survival

BOOK SEVEN

A Different View

W illiam (Bill) J. P. Smith Jr. lived hard. Played hard. Worked hard. During the course of his sixty years he has survived a dysfunctional childhood, the U.S. Marine Corps., the trenches of the advertising/public relations business world, university academic warfare and four wives. Now he would find himself having to survive one more time as a male with a female disease. Breast Cancer.

"I didn't even know men could get breast cancer," he told me. Many men do not know they can get it. There is very little publicity about male breast cancer and very little interest. Bill's treatment was a radical modified mastectomy, tamoxifen, and a lot of talking about it. He wanted to educate the male population. "A lump is a lump is a lump," he says about the lump he had found by his nipple. With only 1,800 men diagnosed a year, male breast cancer isn't a high profile issue. Not many people care. Except a guy like Bill who became determined to talk to his peers about something they didn't want to hear. To him, it was no longer just a woman's battle. It had become his also.

Bill told me his self-image changed after the operation. He had a big dimple in his chest. When he got up each morning, it was there to face him. He longed to share his feelings with other men but they didn't want to talk about it. They didn't know how. It made them uncomfortable. It left Bill with his own discomfort. "I kept thinking, is there a flaw in my masculinity? What will my children's reaction be? What will my fiancee, Linda think? Will I be able to hold a job? What about my sexuality? And what will the "boys" think?" Yet he couldn't discuss his fears, his doubts, his panic with any of his peers. Even when Bill sought professional help, he found his questions couldn't be answered. There were few support groups at the time and few doctors who counseled men with this problem. When Bill started digging for facts, he found there wasn't much research being done on this subject. After all, there are only about 1% of men in the U.S. with breast cancer. It usually is ignored in males, for it's thought of as a woman's disease.

As a breast cancer survivor, Bill entered a woman's world in a new way. Before, he had noticed a woman's walk, her form, her exterior, but now he found himself aware of what she was feeling. It was as if a door had opened and he had stepped into a room never visited before. A room filled with women's feelings, their fears, and their issues. Bill understood for the first time about a body changing, not being as you re-membered it or wanted it. He now understood the shock and the disbelief in hearing the word, "mastectomy." "I never real-ized before how important self-image is to a woman, or to my-self," he admitted. In one of the support groups he attended, someone said, "If you feel deformed, it's hard to feel sexy." He was the only man in the group. For awhile he didn't and couldn't feel sexual. That's when he began to choose his fe-male friends from a different view. What they had to say, what they felt, and what they hoped for became more important. And it was wonderful.

Bill says he now has the privilege to "peek" into a woman's world. He can relate to that world much better now, though he admits he believes that women are the braver of the two species. He realizes that although he didn't see the world com-pletely from a woman's viewpoint, he got very close.

But it's a man's disease he wants to talk about and spread the word. He wants to let men know that breast cancer is not selective. He wants men to have those check-ups and not ig-nore any lumps they might find themselves. He wants fund raisers to include the subject of male breast cancer, and he wants men to be included, not only to support their wives, daughters and girlfriends, but to support themselves as well.

It is seven years since Bill was diagnosed. He is now mar-ried and discovering every day that breast cancer cannot destroy femininity in women, nor masculinity in men.

Unless you let it.

William J. P. Smith Jr. appears in the book, "Living With Breast Cancer… Thirty-Nine Women And One Man Speak Candidly About Surviving Breast Cancer," by Perry Colmore and Lisa Adelsberger

Email Bill at: WJPSJr.@worldnet.att.net

~

Deserving Better

Do not continue if you are over 60. There is nothing here you don't already know.

A woman checks into a senior hotel. She is healthy, bright, eager to live. She sees women sitting all day in housedresses and flees to her son's house. This is not what she wanted or expected. "I'm young yet," she says. "Not ready for that." She is eighty years old. Money is not a problem. Feeling loved and needed is.

Another senior works three days a week. "Work is good for you," he tells me. "It keeps you young. The day I can't work, I don't want to be here." He also admits work isn't a choice. His Social Security check doesn't meet his needs. "How can you live on $900.00 a month today?" he asks. His house is paid off, but there are taxes, insurance, a car. So he rents part of his home. He cannot survive without a salary.

There are more stories. About medical bills that can't be paid. About those who choose not to get their prescriptions renewed because they can't afford them. About the pain in not having the money to live. About the fear when health insurance payments rise. About the anxiety when illness takes control.

"I didn't think it would be like this," a woman close to 70 tells me. "I get sick every time I have to pay the bills." But pay them she does. A little here. A little there. A note that promises something next month. She has children. They love her, but they are busy. The world is busy. We live in a young society, though 62 million are over 50. We are more connected to computers than one another.

But not like my Aunt Betty. She lived in one home, then another, always with a sister or brother. That's the way it was then. She was our Aunt Betty, and it didn't bother her one bit that she shared my room, used my bureau for her clothes, and told me what to do and how to do it. So my mother took her in and her sisters and brothers took her in. She came with suitcases, stayed awhile and complained. And when no one could stand it any longer, she left. We loved Aunt Betty, and her living with us enlarged our personal universe.

As did the man who slept in our kitchen. My father brought him home from work one day. He was new on the job and had nowhere to live. He needed a place to sleep, and that was that. We paid special attention to him and made certain we were quiet so we didn't disturb his kitchen privileges. The reward for washing his clothes and packing a lunch for him came from within. I recall the feeling of connection when he smiled and went on his way.

There was always someone living in my house who wasn't part of the family. I don't know how that came to be. They just needed something and we gave what was needed. Didn't matter what it was. Didn't matter if we didn't have it. We gave it anyway.

Over 60 is a scary place to be. Loneliness in a young society, in a selfish society with a short-term mentality, can be terminal. Lack of income can be the downfall of dignity. It can be brutal. Feeling isolated, unappreciated, at the end of the road, when the traveling promised so much, can be devastating.

So for those about to take this journey into the senior years, pack carefully for the trip. Bring an extra supply of self-respect and fight for it, every mile of the way. Make certain others value your existence and speak out to remind them that you're a privilege, not an obligation. Remind those who forget that the struggle to survive without sufficient funds can be tough enough, but having to beg for help makes it unbearable. Shout if you have to, make as much noise on the road as you can to remind the young that they too will grow old, and the world they create for the aged will be waiting for them. And if you deserve better, demand it, let others know, don't keep it a secret. Ask for help if you need it and if you are rejected, ask again because you deserve it.

You are a source of experience, wisdom, courage, and endurance with a message that needs to be delivered before the journey ends.

Don't make it easy for the world to forget you. More important, don't forget yourself.

—

Heroes

He is 81. She is 78. He was a bombardier in World War II and flew 50 bombing missions. She raised a family of three, worked, and was active in community activities. Now they both are in the war called aging and their battle is being fought with determination.

He must go into the hospital shortly for tests. Seizures have attacked him for years and taken away his ability to use his surf boards and bicycles. He no longer walks the beach alone because the seizures are now more frequent. She too has had her own health problems. We are to spend the day with them and witness the battle being fought… the battle against giving up.

She greets us at the door, dressed in a lovely long gown. We are her company and she is prepared. We are unprepared for the abundance of food that keeps coming to the table. Fruits and salads delivered as we talk. The refrigerator door opens and closes as we say, "No, thank you. We are full." He quips, "You're not finished eating until she breaks you." It returns, the old feeling when families sat around the table for hours, eating and talking, warming each other's spirits.

We are deep in conversation as we eat. We do not stop talking. We talk about the yesterdays and our experiences together. We talk about family. We talk about the present. Politics. Love. Survival. And we keep eating.

Later, he shows us his flowers. He works in the garden every day. "Look at this rose," he says. He cuts it and hands it to me to hold as his wife takes a photograph of us. Immediately after, he says, "I must put it in some water now. You can't let a rose perish." His garden is youthful, filled with vitality. "Next year it will be better," he promises.

And then he shares his other interest. He displays the jewelry he makes. Bracelets. Earrings. Wire pounded into figurines. For those he loves. He's been doing it for years and designs each one himself. He will make me a happy face to hang around my neck. Quickly, on a piece of paper, he sketches how it will look. He draws a face. It is smiling. "The eyes will be green stones," he tells me.

The telephone rings and rings again. Their family calls in, ammunition in the battle against aging. Great-grandchildren. Grandchildren. Children. Friends. The caring comes from the outside and fills the house. "Are you OK?" "Do you need anything?"

They are independent on most days. She still drives and

does the shopping. He still takes out the trash and fixes up things and helps her. They tell us with pride how busy they are between the planting and the cooking and the jewelry-making, and overcoming the next hurdle.

And we go for the walk on the beach one short block away. He is like a young boy, so thrilled to be there again, for since the seizures have increased, he must wait until a guest arrives to accompany him. He talks to everyone. A little boy is building a sand castle. He inspects it carefully. A man is fishing. They discuss what's being caught and what isn't. He picks up seashells from the beach, looking for special ones to save. "Isn't this wonderful?" he asks. "The water on your feet. What could be better?" We see through his eyes, the houses overlooking the beach, the ripples in the waves. He captures each moment, savors it, and we find ourselves doing the same.

And later, we sit outside on the deck, the ocean breeze blending with the rich moments we are sharing.

"Next year you'll come here to the shore house and see a better garden," he promises before we leave. "And soon, I'll send you your happy face."

She has a menu already set for our next visit. In between she will get him to the hospital for tests, do the driving, do the daily things as he will do also. To keep their house going. To keep themselves going.

And if age is waiting to win the battle, it will have to wait much longer.

For this is a war they intend to win.

~

Hope

I did not want to live one more moment after I learned my daughter, Beth, had breast cancer. But had I been granted my wish, I would not have experienced the outpouring of love and support from friends, family, and our community. All too often, we are faced with news that diminishes the value of human beings, that spotlights our dark side, that exaggerates our weaknesses, that gives one the impression that all we are capable of is killing one another and destroying each other's lives. The other side deserves telling also.

From the time two friends cradled me in their arms, love has poured in and set us on our feet. We are a sharing family. We do not keep secrets. We believe in reaching out and in giving. We are not ashamed of the word, "cancer." So it was only natural that we tell others what had happened to shatter our serenity.

I did so through writing. Beth did so through the telephone. My nine-year-old grandson, Ryan, did so by standing up in his class and asking his friends to pray. One classmate gave him a lucky charm. Each of us in the family opened the door to his heart and let anyone in who might nourish it.

Nourishment arrived in abundance. Neighbors brought my daughter dinners, flowers and their survival stories. A friend contributed the third of his miracles. He said that every Scotsman had three. He had used up two. There were prayer chains and offers of help from every direction. Rides. House-cleaning. Cooking. Baby-sitting.

And the survival stories kept coming. One breast cancer survivor after another reached us, urging us to believe in the cure and in the fight. Five years, ten years, fifteen years. Surviving. Living. Working through treatment. People stopped me on the street and shared their experiences. And I wanted to hear everything they had to say. I needed to see the living and the working and hear their laughter. "This is the year 2000," I heard over and over again. "It's different today. We live."

Beth and I have been drafted into the war against breast cancer. We cannot afford self-pity, or consider defeat. There is work to do. People talk of a cure. I want to talk of a cause. Why are so many young women getting breast cancer? In my forties, I did not have one friend who had it. Beth has many and they each know many more. In their thirties and forties. Is it our air? Is it our water? Can we do something to prevent this happening to the next generation? Are we not doing enough? How can we do more?

But even as I seek the answers to these questions, life bravely continues. The Little League season has begun and my grandson is getting ready to play, my son-in-law to coach. A friend calls and asks if I would like to go to a garage sale. I accept. I begin to set the bungalow up for summer rental. Beth frolics on the beach with her six-year-old daughter, Jenny, and they build sand castles. I hear their laughter.

If I had closed my eyes and not awakened when breast cancer entered my daughter's life, I would have missed the chance to grow, to change, and to see that evolution in others. I would have missed the opportunity to join this battle against breast cancer, and to be part of the army that some day will defeat it. As much as I thought I knew in my 66 years, I didn't know enough about this ongoing war and I didn't believe enough in the goodness of the human race.

This experience has taught me that we human beings need to realize how kind we can be, how loving, how giving, how unselfish, how courageous. I learned we have a capability to reach within ourselves and dig for riches beyond our wildest expectations; treasures such as spirit, determination and just plain grit. The good stories about us do not come often enough from the media. The stories about the generosity of people, the kindness to one another, the beautiful healing of love we can offer, the reaching out, the giving, the feeling of common pain, the tears shed and the laughter shared.

We do not read enough about our good side.

This time, you will.

Mothers Supporting Daughters with Breast Cancer, c/o Charmayne S. Dierker, 21710 Bayshore Road, Chestertown, MD 21620-4401, or call 410-778-1982

〜

Moving On

A friend called to tell me she had left her husband of fifteen years. He had been unfaithful. She couldn't forgive his actions. So she packed up her pets, her belongings, and left the state. To find another place to live.

I spoke to her the week before she was to leave. She was frightened. As bad as her situation was at home, she feared the unknown, the leaving, the loneliness. "I'm afraid I won't be able to do it." she told me. "I don't know anyone where I'm going. I'll be there alone. At least with him, I had a life."

It was a life of pain, of unfaithfulness, of disrespect. But she had grown used to it and didn't think she could find anything more. Night after night, she would call, crying, wondering if leaving was the right thing to do, all the while knowing she couldn't return to the situation waiting for her. None of us knew if she would find the courage she needed to move on. As much as we supported her and encouraged her, we knew the final decision had to be hers.

At a Writer's Group where I teach, I asked the participants

to write an essay called, "If I could choose to be someone else, who would that be?" A woman in her eighties wrote, "I wish I could risk more… be a person who takes chances. I was always afraid to do that." But then she added, "Now I don't know what I was afraid of. Whatever happened in life, I always managed to somehow handle it." This woman was thinking of changing her life circumstances, moving from a large house where she was familiar with everything, to a senior citizen community where it would be easier for her to get along. She felt defeated by age and a body that had its limitations.

It is difficult to move on. Everything familiar seems to be left behind. Safe places. Comfort zones. Whether it's a move from a house, or a relationship, it's as if one is stepping out into darkness, where there is no light. Risking is a risky business. When I bought my house at the shore, I left my home of 35 years and the state in which I lived. My new neighbors were strangers; my support group of friends were left behind. It took awhile to feel comfortable in the strange rooms, to look out the window at unfamiliar sights, but gradually, the new sights became old ones and the unfamiliar became comfortable.

After 67 years of moving on, now I am again afraid. I know I have to make some changes in my life, take some chances, move in a direction that holds no certainty. One foot refuses to step in front of the other.

Recently I heard from the woman who left her husband. She has relocated. "It is difficult," she says. Sometimes she is very lonely. But she has done things to lessen the emptiness. She joined a local support group. She loves animals. She volunteered at the local zoo. She is looking for a job.

Instead of moving, the 81-year-old woman risked by staying. She had a bathroom put on the first floor, and she will sleep in a small spare room. She has changed her house, her living conditions, her attitude, so that she can stay in the neighborhood she has lived in all her life. And in doing so, is moving on.

My one-year-old grandson Ben, stands on his feet and for the first time, tries to walk. His legs are hesitant. He isn't certain if they can hold his body up or take him where he wants to go. But there is something across the room Ben wants and he can't resist trying to get there. So little by little, step by step, he begins his journey, short to our adult eyes, but very long to his infant ones. He doesn't quite make it the first time, but he gets right up and tries again. And again. He doesn't entertain the idea of failure.

I will try to follow his example.

~

Trailblazers

I meet trailblazers every week when I attend the Senior Citizen Center. They are not athletes or entertainers. They are not people in the spotlight. They do not stand on stages and receive awards or gifts for their services. They are rarely written about. Nobody gives them a ticker tape parade. Most of them are over 55. Most of them could tell you a lot about life's twists and turns. And how to survive them. If anybody has the time to listen.

A woman tells me she works in a gift shop. Some might think it's nothing special. This woman, who starts her day early in the morning is seventy years old. She is not young and vigorous as she once was. But the job is necessary to supplement her income. She wants to support herself and take nothing from her family. And so she works hard, standing on her feet much longer than they enjoy. Her body rebels. It resents the long hours and the physical stress. But the woman tells me she must be independent in order to keep her self- respect.

And so she works beyond her own expectations, daring to stretch her horizons.

A man who recently lost his wife after 60 years of marriage, says he lost everything. He says he could find no reason to go on. He felt living was over for him. He had a good life with a good woman. His children are grown. His useful days, he thought, were finished. But now he fills his free time volunteering at a local school, reading to young people. They write him notes of thanks and hug him. They say they miss him when there are vacations and the school is closed. He is needed there. And so he goes on appreciating life. Re-discovering it.

A long-time member of the Center passes on. Many attend her funeral. She was a poet and wrote often of the group that was important to her. Poem after poem. Her family put all her poetry in an album and presented it to the Center. Each week, someone reads her work in tribute to her talent and to her caring.

They face the passing away of many friends, the members changing, as illness and death claim their victims, and yet there continues to be a celebration of life. In spite of it all, they come each week, they greet each other with hugs and news, they work at replacing the fear and loneliness with socializing and giving, and they bite the bullet when it comes to dealing with the daily reminders of aging.

Those in advanced age are dealing every day with loneliness, physical pain, financial stress, a world that is in the express lane and has no patience for those traveling in the slower one, and a society that is working at remaining young. And yet each day offers the opportunity to do something they have never done before. Travel. Collect sea glass. Run for political office. Join a theater group, an exercise course. Or fall in love again. Older adults can explore all of it, as long as the spirit for adventure remains strong and the pioneer in them remains undaunted.

A woman in her eighties is on chemotherapy. She is fighting back. Some think that at her age, the fight might be gone. But it isn't. She is planning a full recovery. She has things to do. Going to the Center is one of them. Helping others less fortunate is another. Pride in the victory will be hers. Just the way a marathon runner feels when he crosses the finish line and the crowd applauds. Age doesn't take that away. The desire to win. The eagerness to learn. The need to love. At the Center they applaud one another, for they appreciate what it takes to get through each day and to add something valuable to it.

They are called senior citizens. I call them trailblazers. They have come through world wars, depressions, epidemics. And just when they thought they would be able to take it easy, and perhaps enjoy the benefits of their hard work, they find themselves with an extra 20 years of life expectancy, not enough money for the journey, and a body that didn't know it had another twenty miles to go. In the midst of all this, they are expected to make changes, give up lifestyles, pitch in, butt out, look good, and be eternally pleasant so that they are not labeled "old goats."

Who were these people when they were younger? Executives. Business people. Housewives. Mothers. Teachers. Artists. They had titles and were identified by what they did. If they worked in the home or at the office, they filled a role. But now identities have been discarded. Age becomes the common denominator. Who they were doesn't seem to matter. Who they are matters much more to each other and to whomever recognizes the richness, the wisdom, and the pure grit offered by those in advanced age.

If their generation is the first to live longer, then they are also the first to do it with limitless possibilities.

They are the trailblazers of the 21st century.

~

About the Author

Harriet May Savitz was born in Newark, New Jersey, and grew up during the depression. Watching her father lose everything and spend the rest of his life trying to recapture a dream, she realized the magic of fantasy and began a dream of her own. At age nine, Harriet wrote her first poem, and to the delight of thousands of readers, she hasn't put her pen down since.

Mrs. Savitz is a co-founder of the Philadelphia Children's Reading Round Table and is the author of over 21 books for young adults. She quickly became an award-winning author of this genre, with one of her books adapted by Henry Winkler Productions for an ABC After School Special.

Several years ago, her voice began speaking to adults in personal, inspiring essays through which the reader is able to get in touch with the richness, wisdom, and pure grit of this woman who meets and writes about life's challenges with a gutsy, uplifting attitude. Two books of these essays, *"Growing Up At 62,"* and *"Messages from Somewhere: Inspiring Stories of*

Life After 60," have been published by Little Treasure Publications. In addition, these life-enhancing essays can be found in newspaper columns and magazines, both local and national, and Ezines (On-line magazines).

Mrs. Savitz is a contributing author for the bestsellers, *"Chicken Soup for the Golden Soul"* and *"Chicken Soup for the Sports Fan's Soul,"* as well as the Chocolate Series.

You can also find her work on numerous web sites, including www.harrietmaysavitz.com and www.littletreasurebooks.com. Her work is housed in The deGrummond Collection, University Libraries, McCain Library & Archives in Hattiesburg, Mississippi.

~

LITTLE TREASURE PUBLICATIONS, INC.

www.littletreasurebooks.com

The company that publishes books to be remembered

Etchings of the Soul

~

Tincture of Tears and Laughter

~

Rising to the Dawn:
A Rape Survivor's Journey Into Healing

~

Growing up at 62

~

Echoes of a Voice Within

~

Messages from Somewhere:
Inspiring Stories of Life After 60

~

Coming Soon – Our first book for children:
Tiny Red's Trip to Earth

Messages from Somewhere

Wisdom…

Memoirs . . .

Challenges . . .

Turning Points . . .

Milestones . . .

Renewal . . .

Inspiring Stories of Life After 60

Harriet May Savitz